INSURANCE LEA

INSURANCES OF LIABILITY

by

CAROL S. C. BENNETT

LONDON
WITHERBY & CO. LTD.
32-36 Aylesbury Street,
London EC1R 0ET
Telephone 01-251 5341
Fax No. 01-251 1296

1st Edition 1984
2nd Edition 1989

MONUMENT
SERIES

©

WITHERBY & CO. LTD.

1989

ISBN 0 948691 67 0

CONTENTS

INTRODUCTION

'Insurance Learners' were introduced in 1984 as a valuable study aid for the Qualifying Examination of the Chartered Insurance Institute. These 'slim volumes' aim to serve both as preliminary *reading and revision texts*. The Learner series has been widely acclaimed and clearly fulfils the authors' intended purpose. They help the student organise his or her thoughts and gain insight into the study material before moving on to the main text which should be studied more effectively as a result. Once the main text has been completed, frequent revision should be undertaken with the aid of the Learner whose design facilitates this approach. The publisher and author believe that the Learner is most effective when used in conjunction with the relevant main text published by the CII Tuition Service.

The CII kindly allows the reproduction of an examiners report but the student is advised to obtain copies relating to other years of the same examination. The author is most grateful to his wife, Maureen, for her patience and assistance in preparing the manuscript.

How the "Learner" should be used

The "Learner" is more than just a crammer — rather it is a succinct complement to a planned programme of study and a valuable revision aid. You should:

1) Locate the topic to be studied in the "Learner" and read it.

2) Read the topic as covered by the main CII textbook and as directed by the lecturer if attending a class.

   Note taking from the main text, and during oral tuition should be easier and more effective now that the "Learner" has opened up the topic area. area.

3) Re-read the topic in the "Learner", revising frequently from your notes and the Learner.

CHAPTER 1

LEGAL LIABILITIES

THE NATURE OF A LIABILITY POLICY

1.1   **A liability policy** provides an indemnity in respect of legal liability to pay compensation to others. Damage or injury to others or their property is not enough in itself to make the insured liable even though an involvement arises by way of accident or otherwise. Thus, whenever an occurrence of claims potential arises, the insurer must consider:

(a)   does the policy apply to the circumstances, injury, or damage of the stated case?

(b)   was the insured legally liable for the injury/damage?

Even if it transpires that no legal liability attaches to the insured, if (a) is answered in the affirmative the insured will benefit from the services rendered by the insurer in defending allegations against him.

Liabilities that concern the policies described below arise in tort, in contract, or under statute.

Tort

1.2   **Tort is a civil wrong,** arising by operation of the law, the remedy for which is a claim for unliquidated damages (i.e. awarded at the court's discretion and not fixed as a covenanted pre-estimate for an anticipated breach of contract). Tort is commonly about collisions and invasions arising from the breach of recognised duties. Breach of contract and tort can overlap. An accountant, for example, owes his client a duty of care which is implied in contract and arises in tort. In contract the duties are assumed by agreement, express or implied.

1.3   **Tort is distinguished from crime** by the consequences of the act itself and not the act itself. In tort, a remedy (e.g. damages) is sought for the plaintiff. In crime the emphasis is upon punishment of the offender rather than compensation for the aggrieved. The same wrong (e.g. reckless driving) may give rise to both civil proceedings, e.g. an action for damages by an injured party, and criminal prosecution. In fact, torts, breaches of contract and crimes are not necessarily mutually exclusive.

1.4   **THE PRINCIPAL TORTS**
The main torts are negligence, nuisance, trespass, defamation, and strict liability. Exhibit 1 sets out a very broad guide which relates the main torts to the principal interests that they protect.

1

EXHIBIT 1 — THE PRINCIPAL TORTS

TORT	PRINCIPAL INTERESTS PROTECTED
Negligence	Damage/injury caused by careless physical invasions.
Nuisance	Interference with real property.
Trespass	Wilful, direct physical invasions of persons or property.
Wrongful interference with goods	Interference with personal goods.
Defamation	Interference with a person's reputation.

In addition, there is a variety of interests protected by those matters and obligations that are the subject of strict liability and statute.

CHAPTER 2

NEGLIGENCE

2.1 **Negligence** — 'the omission to do something a *reasonable* and prudent man would do, or doing something a prudent and reasonable man would not do' — Blyth v. Birmingham Waterworks (1856). The test is *objective*, i.e. a person is not judged by what he considers reasonable but what a reasonable person would or would not do in particular circumstances.

2.2 **Who is the reasonable man?** — Eloquent phrases have been used to describe him. He is well-known as the 'man on the Clapham omnibus'. He does not 'have to possess the wisdom of a Hebrew prophet or the agility of an acrobat'. Thus, a person is not an insurer of his fellow men — to be liable, he must be at **fault**. Fault in this context means failure to live up to the standard of a reasonable man. The law does not excuse inexperience. In *Nettleship v. Weston (1971)*, a learner driver's inexperience was not excused. However, in cases involving professional skills, the required standard of care is that of 'the ordinary skilled man exercising and professing to have that skill'. Accordingly, a surgeon must bring to his tasks the skill of the ordinary practitioner of that branch of medicine. If a professional claims to have skill and expertise above that of the ordinary practitioner it seems reasonable to expect him to show the standard of skill and expertise he claimed to possess.

2.3 **The constituents of negligence.** To succeed in an action, the plaintiff must clear 'three hurdles', i.e. show that:

(a) the defendant **owed the plaintiff a duty of** care.

(b) the defendant was in **breach of his duty**.

(c) the plaintiff **sustained damage as a result** provided that the **damage was not too remote**.

2.4 **DUTY OF CARE**
The English law's fault requirement appears to have its origin in a reluctance to impose liability. Lord Denning said that requiring the plaintiff to show that he was owed a duty of care was 'simply a way of limiting the range of liability for negligence'. Many plaintiffs have failed because of their inability to establish the existence of a duty of care. The problem of clearing 'the duty hurdle' was at its greatest prior to 1932 (see 2.5 below) when the plaintiff needed to show that he had something in the nature of a formalised relationship with the defendant such as: employer/employee; highway users/adjacent occupiers of premises; occupiers/visitors. An employee, for example, could show that his employer owed him a duty to take reasonable care to prevent injury arising out of the employment.

2.5   **The neighbour principle.** A lady, having drunk the contents of an opaque ginger beer bottle which contained the decomposed remains of a snail, suffered gastro-enteritis as a result. She could not sue the retailer for breach of contract (i.e. failure to supply a product fit for human consumption) as, not having purchased the product, she had no contractual relationship with the retailer. Her companion had made the purchase. A further difficulty was that she did not stand in any previously recognised formal relationship with the manufacturer whereby the latter owed her a duty of care. The resultant landmark case, *Donoghue v. Stevenson (1932)* brought Lord Atkin to formulate a general duty of care while also creating a new category of duty — manufacturer and consumer. Lord Atkin said:

> 'you must take reasonable care to avoid acts or omissions likely to injure your neighbour'. Neighbours are 'persons . . . so closely and directly affected by my act that I ought reasonably to have them in contemplation as being so affected when . . . directing my mind to the acts or omissions called into question'.

2.6   **Reasonable contemplation**, therefore, may be sufficient to create a duty of care and moves the matter well beyond the limitation imposed by formal relationships.

2.7   **Neighbour principle reaffirmed.** This was by Lord Wilberforce in *Anns v. London Borough of Merton (1978)*. In considering the extent of the principle, two points emerged:

(a)   If there is a sufficient relationship of proximity or neighbourhood such that in the reasonable contemplation of the defendant, carelessness on his part, may be likely to cause damage to the plaintiff, then a prima facie case arises.

(b)   It is then necessary to consider whether there are any considerations which ought to negative or reduce or limit the scope of the duty or class of person to whom it is owed for the damage to which the breach of it may give rise.

2.8   **A question of law.** The existence of a duty is a question of law and the law has restricted the scope of the duty sometimes because of the type of damage (e.g. economic loss). Also certain plaintiffs have been designated as 'unforeseeable' because of the way in which the damage occurred or, perhaps, because of their position (see 2.10).

2.9   **THE SCOPE OF THE DUTY**
The extent of the duty depends on:

(a)   reasonable foresight.

(b)   reasonable care.

If a man can reasonably foresee that his acts may cause injury or damage to his neighbour, he must use reasonable care to avoid it. In *Haley v. L.E.B. (1965)*, the plaintiff, who was blind, fell into the defendants' excavation. They should have foreseen the presence of the blind in the locality and used something better than a sloping punner hammer to protect them.

4

2.10   Unforeseeable plaintiffs is a term that has been applied to plaintiffs outside the duty area. In *Bourhill v. Young (1941)* — the case of the pregnant fishwife — a careless motor-cyclist collided with a vehicle and died. The plaintiff was in the vicinity but, being shielded by a tram car, was not exposed to the risk of being struck or actually seeing the accident. She heard the collision and saw blood on the road. She suffered nervous shock and miscarried. The House of Lords held that the defendant could not have foreseen any injury to a person in her position.

In *Palsgraf v. Long Island Railway (1928)* the defendants' servants carelessly dislodged a parcel containing fireworks. The ensuing explosion knocked over some scales twenty-five feet distant where they struck the plaintiff. It was held that there was no liability as the plaintiff was 'unforeseeable'.

2.11   Types of damage not always covered by the duty. At one time it appeared that the duty of care was limited to the avoidance of personal injury and loss/damage to property. In particular the law has been reluctant to impose a duty in the following cases:

(a)   nervous shock.

(b)   economic loss resulting from negligent statements.

(c)   economic loss resulting from negligent acts.

2.12   LIABILITY FOR NERVOUS SHOCK
The reluctance to award damages has been attributed to:

(a)   claims of this type being difficult to verify.

(b)   possible prospect of creating a liability out of all proportion to the defendant's negligence.

(c)   the 'floodgates' principle, i.e. the undesirability of a proliferation of claims.

Shock is capable of affecting a wide range and, apparently, it was felt necessary to impose limitations on the extent of the admissible claims.

2.13   The developing nature of nervous shock claims.

(a)   There must normally be a **definite illness** (e.g. psychoneurosis which is verifiable). There is no liability for grief and sorrow, but damages for 'ordinary shock' were awarded in *Whitmore v. Euroways Express Coaches & Ors. (1984).*

(b)   There is liability for shock which:

   (i)   **accompanies physical injury**.

   (ii)   results from the plaintiff having been put in **fear of physical injury**. (In *Dulieu v. White (1901)* a barmaid escaped physical injury by way of contact when confronted by a horsedrawn vehicle which unexpectedly entered her workplace but there was liability for shock.)

(c) A claim is admissible for nervous shock brought on by **injury, or fear thereof, to a near relative** when the plaintiff is in **'the disaster area'** within sight or sound of the immediate injury or threat thereof. In *Hambrook v. Stokes Bros. (1925)*, S's negligence caused an unattended lorry to go down a hill towards a place where Mrs. H's children had gone. The lorry went out of sight round a bend. Later Mrs. H. was told that a child had been injured. She suffered shock but damages were awarded on the basis of what she saw and not what she was told. In *Hinz v. Berry (1970)* a widow was awarded damages for the shock sustained when she witnessed the death of her husband and injury to her children. The family car was parked in a lay-by when struck by the defendant's car. Mrs. Hinz observed the tragedy from a nearby field where she was picking flowers.

(d) Damages can also be awarded for shock sustained by a relative who, not seeing or hearing the incident, came upon it in the **immediate aftermath**. In *Boardman v. Sanderson (1964)*, the defendant reversed his car into the plaintiff's son. The defendant, knowing that the plaintiff was nearby, should have contemplated that injury to the son was likely to bring the father to the scene and so expose him to the risk of injury by nervous shock. In *Marshall v. Lionel Enterprise (1972)*, the mother was at home one hundred yards away but on news of an accident ran to the scene and there suffered shock.

(e) It appears that a rescuer, who suffers shock in the rescue necessitated by the defendant's negligence, has an admissible claim — *Chadwick v. British Railways Board (1967)*. *Wigg v. British Rail Board (1986)*.

(f) The above cases involve plaintiffs within the disaster area at the relevant time and so exposed to the risk of shock by sight or sound or by coming quickly to the scene in the 'immediate aftermath' of the event. The case of *McLoughlin v. O'Brian (1982)* shows that the 'scene' does not necessarily have to be that of the accident and that 'aftermath' is a term not necessarily confined to minutes. Mrs. McLoughlin's family was in a road accident two miles away. Two hours later she went to the hospital and saw them in very distressing circumstances. The House of Lords held that the shock she suffered was a reasonably foreseeable consequence of the negligence of the lorry drivers involved. The House of Lords rejected the view of the Court of Appeal that public policy limited the duty of care.

2.14 **Elements to be considered in nervous shock claims.** In McLoughlin's case, Lord Wilberforce stated that the three elements to be considered are:

(a) **Class of persons.** When the plaintiff himself does not suffer injury or threat, the relationship with the injured or threatened party becomes important. This may range from the closest family tie (e.g. parent/child, husband/wife) to the mere bystander. The first class, subject to the other considerations, is likely to have an admissible claim. The second will not unless, as in Chadwick's case, the circumstances invite rescue; persons of this class are either expected to have sufficient fortitude to enable them to endure the calamities of life, or, the reason is that the defendants cannot be expected to compensate the world at large. The closer the plaintiff is to the first class the better will be the prospects for a successful claim.

(b) **Proximity to the accident.** There must be closeness in time and in space, but to insist on direct sight and hearing is impractical and unjust. The 'aftermath' doctrine should ensure that those, like Mrs. McLoughlin, who come quickly to the distress, should not be excluded.

(c) **Means of causing shock.** The law does not compensate for shock brought about by third party communication. The shock must come from sight, sound, or aftermath.

2.15 The test of liability for nervous shock. This is reasonable foreseeability of injury to the plaintiff through nervous shock resulting from the defendant's negligence. It remains to be seen whether liability arises for nervous shock arising from damage or threat thereof to property. *Attia v. British Gas* is pending and is outlined in the C.I.I. Journal 12/2.

2.16 ECONOMIC LOSS RESULTING FROM NEGLIGENT STATEMENTS
A negligent (mis)statement may lead to personal injury or property damage but the most common damage following misstatement is economic loss. This book is not concerned with deliberate misstatements which amount to the tort of deceit. It concentrates on negligent misstatements. There used to be no liability in the absence of a contractual or fiduciary relationship. In *Candler v. Crane Christmas & Co. (1951)*, the plaintiff lost the investment he was prompted to make after reading a company's financial statements negligently produced by the defendant accountants acting on behalf of the company with a view to procuring the investment. The plaintiff was not a client of the accountants so no question of breach of contract arose; neither could the plaintiff succeed in tort as it was held that the accountants owed him no duty of care. The reluctance to award damages in such cases has been explained as follows:

(a) the statement may not have been intended as the basis for action.

(b) 'words travel faster than deeds' and could lead to excessive liability.

(c) careless statements should be treated differently to careless acts.

2.17 Hedley Byrne extends the duty of care
In *Hedley Byrne v. Heller & Partners (1963)*, the House of Lords overruled *Cander v. Crane, Christmas & Co. (1951)* removing the distinction between physical damage and pure economic (i.e. financial) loss whenever a 'special relationship' exists. Hedley Byrne, advertising agents, asked their bank to check the creditworthiness of E. & Co. Ltd. who had asked them to place television advertising contracts. Hedley Byrne took this precaution in anticipation, in accordance with trade practice, of accepting responsibility for payment to the television companies relying on recovering their outlay from their clients. Heller & Partners, bankers of E. & Co. Ltd., gave a reference to the effect that the latter could meet their normal commitments. Hedley Byrne relied upon this statement, which proved unsound, and lost £17,000. The House of Lords held that the defendants owed a duty of care in connection with such statements but had, by use of the term 'without responsibility', exempted themselves from liability. Nonetheless a principle had been established, although liability depends on a 'special relationship' not mere foreseeability. To summarise, the position now is that:

'Whenever a **special relationship** exists, there arises a duty to take care in the making of statements, a breach of which would found liability for the harm suffered unless there was a **disclaimer of responsibility**.'

The key elements are 'special relationship' and 'no disclaimer'.

The following questions are invariably relevant in enquiring into the existence of a special relationship:

(a)   Was it reasonable for the plaintiff to rely on the person making the statement because of special knowledge or skill?

(b)   Did the defendant claim special knowledge or skill or conduct a relevant business or profession? The 'Hedley Byrne' principle is not, it seems, restricted to the advice given in the ordinary course of the adviser's business contrary to *Mutual Life & Citizen's Assurance v. Evatt (1971)*.

(c)   Did the defendant know, or should he have known, that his statement would be relied upon by the plaintiff?

(d)   Was the statement made in a 'business context'?

2.18   Other questions may be relevant depending on the circumstances. E.g. *Anderson & Sons Ltd. v. Rhodes (Liverpool) Ltd. (1967)* the defendant's financial interest in the matter covered by the statement. In the Hedley Byrne case affirmative answers arise to all questions (a) to (d) above, but the disclaimer defeated the plaintiff. Some cases are clearly outside the rule, e.g. advice from an architect while watching extra time in an F.A. Cup Final. The context in which the statement is made was closely scrutinised in *Chaudhry v. Prabhakar & Anr. (1988)*, Times Law Report, 8 June 1988.

The Court of Appeal held that a person who, at the request of a friend found a second-hand car for sale and advised the friend to buy it, knowing that she was relying on his skill and judgment, owed her a duty of care, and would be liable for any misstatement concerning the car if reliance was placed on the statement and loss suffered thereby. Prabhakar acted as an unpaid agent for the plaintiff and, in consequence, the duty of care arose in tort. The fact that principal and agent were friends did not affect the existence of a duty but might affect the degree or standard of care. However, the giving of advice in the context of family, domestic or social context does not of itself create a duty as this must take account of all the circumstances in which the advice is sought or given. In the present case, the creation of a contract between the plaintiff and the car seller was regarded by Stuart-Smith L.J. as powerful evidence that the matter was not purely social and had a business connection. The relationship between the plaintiff and the defendant was considered equivalent to contract save only for the absence of consideration. (The importance of the enquiry in (d) above is thus shown.)

2.19   **Hedley Byrne may overlap with contract.** In *Esso v. Mardon (1975)*, Mardon was induced to sign a lease by a negligent statement which overestimated the expected volume of sales from the leased premises. Esso were held liable for negligence following the petrol station proprietor's insolvency.

2.20 **Immunities**
Barristers do not contract with those they represent and can only be sued in tort, but they enjoy immunity in the conduct of litigation. Judges are not liable for negligence in the performance of their duties. Arbitrators are not liable to the arbitrating parties but an architect when certifying to his client that a stage of building work had been properly completed, was not an arbitrator and therefore not immune. *Sutcliffe v. Thackrah (1974).*

2.21 **ECONOMIC LOSS RESULTING FROM NEGLIGENT ACTS**
Until recently no liability arose in negligence for purely economic loss. There was a fear of creating opened liability — 'liability in an indeterminate amount, for an indeterminate time, to an indeterminate class'.

2.22 For the purpose of illustration, cases are divided into two groups:

(a) **Damaged property not owned by the plaintiff**
Weller v. Foot & Mouth Disease Research Institute (1965). Auctioneers could not recover the financial loss suffered when, following negligence of the defendant, an outbreak of foot and mouth disease caused the closure of the cattle market.

Electrochrome v. Welsh Plastics Ltd. (1968). A lorry negligently damaged a fire hydrant causing the water supply to E's factory to be suspended. A day's work was lost but no recovery could be made as E's loss was purely economic. E, not being the owners of the hydrant or water main, were owed no duty of care.

(b) **Damaged property owned by the plaintiff**
The difference here resides in the long-established duty to take care not to damage other people's property. Damage for want of care will make the defendant liable for that damage and the economic loss flowing from it. In *Spartan Steel & Alloys v. Martin & Co. (Contractors) (1972)* the negligent cutting of a cable interrupted the power supply to the plaintiff's factory. The claim was for:

(i) £368 — metal being processed.

(ii) £400 — profit lost on that metal.

(iii) £1,767 being the profit that would have been made on further lots of metal that, but for the interruption, would have been processed.

Claims (i) and (ii) were allowed as they flowed directly out of damage to property owned by the plaintiff, but (iii), being purely economic loss, was disallowed.

2.23 Recovery for purely economic loss still very restricted

Liability for nervous shock has been assimilated within the principles applying to other forms of loss but little has changed in financial loss cases. The leading case is *Junior Books Ltd. v. The Veitchi Co. Ltd. (1982)*. The defendants, specialist sub-contractors, were negligent in laying a floor in the plaintiff's premises. Having been engaged by the main contractors, the defendants did not themselves have a contract with the plaintiffs. The floor cracked but created no risk of injury or damage to property of the plaintiff. The resultant loss was purely economic consisting of £50,000 for replacing the floor and £150,000 for other financial losses which included the removal of machinery and loss of profits during the interruption consequent upon the re-laying of the floor. The defendants contended that they owed no duty of care and that a finding against them would open the floodgates. Applying Lord Wilberforce's test (see 2.7), the majority in the House of Lords held:

(a) there was the requisite degree of proximity so that the defendants should have known what products were required and that the plaintiffs were relying upon their skill and experience. Also the defendants should have foreseen that negligence on their part would necessitate remedial work and associated economic loss. The relationship fell just short of a contractual one but was sufficiently proximate to create a duty of care.

(b) on the facts there were no policy or other reasons to restrict the duty.

2.24 The exceptional nature of Junior Books

Junior Books appears to have been a truly exceptional case and it seems unlikely that the proximity test will be applied in such a way that it extends the duty beyond the strongest facts. In *Leigh & Sillivan v. Aliakmon Shipping Co. Ltd. (1986)* a negligent carrier was not liable for the pure economic loss of the consignee who did not yet own the goods. In *Muirhead v. Industrial Tank Specialities Ltd. & Ors. (1985)* the first defendants contracted to supply a tank, the tank needed a pump which, in turn, needed an electric motor. The motor had the wrong voltage and this caused the motor to cut out and the loss of lobsters stored in the tank. The third defendants, who supplied the motor, were liable in tort for economic loss consequent upon physical damage (i.e. destruction of the lobsters) but not for any other pure economic loss. The latter included the loss of profit on the operation as a whole. In Muirhead's case the chain of supply involved at least four intermediaries and there was no 'very close proximity' between the plaintiff and the manufacturer of the pump. It also seems that in Spartan Steel type cases (accidents between strangers) there will be no liability for pure economic loss caused by the negligent act. A useful account of liability for economic loss is given in C.I.I. Journal 11/2 at page 81 and Journal 12/3 (p. 165). Further indications of the restricted nature of Junior Books are given in accounts of *Simaan General Contracting Co. v. Pilkington Glass Ltd. (1988)* and *Greater Nottingham Co-operative Society v. Cementation Piling & Foundations Ltd. & Ors. (1988)*.

2.25 BREACH OF DUTY

Once it is shown that a duty exists, it has to be decided how much care has to be exercised. The test is objective in that the defendant will be judged by whether he acted reasonably in the circumstances in which he found himself. Each case turns on its own facts.

2.26 **Establishing a breach of duty**
The court is guided by the following:

(a) **Foreseeability of the risk.** 'People must guard against reasonable probabilities not fantastic possibilities' — *Fardon v. Harcourt-Rivington (1932).* A normally docile dog jumped up and damaged a car window. In *Bolton v. Stone (1951)* the plaintiff was injured by a cricket ball struck out of the ground, a rare occurrence which happened only six times in thirty years. There was insufficient probability to prompt a reasonable man to guard against that risk. On some occasions a reasonable man will, however, guard against rare risks. In *Carmarthenshire C.C. v. Lewis (1955)* a lorry driver was killed when he swerved to avoid a four year old who had wandered out of school. No child had previously strayed in that way but the type of accident was reasonably foreseeable.

(b) **Magnitude of the risk**
The degree of care must be commensurate with the risk confronting the defendant. Two factors arise:

   (i)   seriousness of the injury risked.

   (ii) the likelihood of it occurring.

   The more grievous the injury or the more likely the accident the greater will be the care required — in *Paris v. Stepney B.C. (1951)* a one-eyed welder did not get the proportionate degree of care his condition necessitated.

(c) **Importance of the object to be attained**
It is unreasonable to create a risk for a disproportionate object but an equal risk for a better cause may be justified. Rail speeds could be reduced and so reduce the risk and severity of accidents but at a cost in terms of public convenience. Consequently running trains at normal inter-city speeds is not usually negligent. In *Latimer v. A.E.C. (1953)* the defendants would have safeguarded the plaintiff had they closed down their factory after heavy rainfall had made the floor slippery. However, they had done enough in laying down the sawdust so far as supplies would permit. In *Watt v. Hertfordshire C.C. (1954)* a fireman, injured in an emergency, received no damages as the saving of life justifies risks not normally undertaken.

(d) **General Practice**
A defendant can 'clear his feet' by having acted in accordance with the general and approved practice, but deviation from such practice may be justified. Also the general practice may not be sufficient, i.e. there could be circumstances where a reasonable person would have taken more precautions.

2.27 **DAMAGE MUST NOT BE TOO REMOTE**
Damnum sine injuria (injury without liability) — a person is not necessarily liable for the harm he inflicts. For example, damage may be too remote.

2.28 Damage may be too remote. If a negligent car driver knocks down and injures a pedestrian, the causal link between negligence and injury is normally easy to prove. Some cases are complicated and the chain of causation linking the defendant's negligence with the damage may be such that the court refuses to regard it as sufficiently continuous to attach liability to the defendant. Moreover, the chain may be broken by an intervening cause (novus actus interveniens). It is important to understand the following tests of causation:

- the old test of **directness**.

- the new test of **reasonable foreseeability**.

(i) **The old test of directness**
   The defendant was liable for all the direct and immediate consequences of his wrongful act. In *Polemis and Furness, Withy & Co. (1921)* a plank was negligently knocked into the hold of the ship causing a spark to ignite petrol vapour escaping from defective tins. The fire destroyed the ship whose charterers were liable for the damage as it resulted directly from the negligence even though the outcome could not reasonably have been foreseen.

(ii) **The test of reasonable foreseeability**
   The leading case is the *Wagon Mound-(Overseas Tankship v. Morts Dock & Engineering Co. Ltd. (1961))*. The appellants, charterers of the Wagon Mound, negligently allowed the escape of oil in Sydney Harbour. They could not reasonably have foreseen that oil might ignite when floating on water. It was ignited by sparks from welding work of the respondents who ran a business on a wharf. Considerable damage resulted. Held — appellants not liable as they could not reasonably have foreseen the damage. Polemis was overruled and reasonable foreseeability is accepted as the correct test.

Application of the test
The test applies:

(a) to the type of damage and not its amount.

(b) in a general way to the kind of thing that occurred.

If the **type of damage is foreseeable** the defendant will be liable even though its extent may not have been. In *Smith v. Leech Brain & Co. (1961)* an employee suffered a burn on the lip when splashed by molten metal. Such an injury was foreseeable but it could not have been foreseen that the burn would activate a pre-cancerous condition causing his death. This case illustrates the 'egg-shell' skull rule and shows that directness still has a relevance. Once it is shown that the type of injury is foreseeable, the defendant will be liable for the direct consequences even though unexpected. A tortfeasor 'takes his victim as he finds him'.

   Even negligence of a third party will not break the chain of causation if the type of harm is foreseeable. R slipped on his employer's oily ladder. An anti-tetanus injection administered by a doctor brought on encephalitis for which the employer was liable. The employer could reasonably have foreseen the likelihood of medical attention resulting from their negligence.

The general approach
This means that the defendant is not excused simply because the unexpected arises out of the sort of harm that was foreseeable in a general way. In *Hughes v. Lord Advocate (1963)* there was liability for fire caused by an explosion which, unlike a conflagration, was unexpected and unforeseeable. The plaintiff suffered burns.

In *Bradford v. Robinson Rentals (1967)* frostbite, very rare in England, was the unexpected outcome of the plaintiff's 500 mile journey in a heater-less van during severe weather. The defendants were liable as frostbite was within the general class of risk arising from exposure to severe weather.

In the two preceding cases, the accident was merely a variant of the perils arising unlike the case of *Doughty v. Turner Manufacturing Co. Ltd. (1964)*. In this case an asbestos cement cover was knocked into very hot molten liquid unexpectedly injuring the plaintiff by explosion and not by splashing. In the prevailing state of knowledge an explosion was not foreseeable. Held — no liability as this was a different risk not a mere variant of the perils of splashing.

2.29 PROOF OF NEGLIGENCE — RES IPSA LOQUITUR
The plaintiff must normally prove the defendant's negligence but sometimes 'the facts speak for themselves' — res ipsa loquitur. In *Scott v. London & St. Catherine's Dock Co. (1865)*, S was injured when bags of sugar, without apparent cause, fell from the upper part of the warehouse.

The effect of res ipsa loquitur, which is a rule of evidence, is that negligence is presumed and the onus is on the defendant to disprove it.

The defendant may rebut the presumption by:

(a) showing the actual cause of the damage and that it was consistent with care on his part;

(b) showing that he took reasonable care so that the court may infer that the damage had some other cause. A defendant, unable to show that he took reasonable care, will not rebut the presumption by showing that the damage could have had an alternative cause.

2.30 The conditions for res ipsa loquitur

(a) The event must be one that does not ordinarily occur without negligence (i.e. a presumption of negligence).

(b) The thing (e.g. bags of sugar in Scott's case above) must have been under the exclusive control of the defendant.

(c) There must have been an 'absence of explanation'. In *Barkway v. S. Wales Transport Co. Ltd. (1950)*, B was injured when a bus left the road. The bus had a defective tyre. When all the facts are known, the plaintiff must use them and not rely on res ipsa.

2.31 Some res ipsa cases

Byrne v. Boadle (1863) — Plaintiff was injured by bags of flour falling from a building. This does not ordinarily happen without negligence so satisfying (a) above. The thing (flour) was under the control of the defendant (satisfying (b) above). No explanation was available to the plaintiff ((c) above).

Ellor v. Selfridge (1930) — A motor car mounted the pavement and hit the plaintiff in the back.

EXHIBIT 2

NEGLIGENCE
(Three elements)

| Duty of Care | Breach of Duty | Plaintiff suffered damage in consequence of breach, provided damage ... not too remote |

DUTY OF CARE

(a) Formalising of obligations
(b) Neighbour principle
(c) Reasonable foreseeability — a criterion
(d) A question of law

SCOPE OF THE DUTY

Extent: (a) Reasonable foresight *Haley v. L.E.B. (1965)*
(b) Reasonable care

UNFORESEEABLE
PLAINTIFFS
Bourhill v. Young (1941)
Palsgraff v. Long Island
Railroad (1928)

NERVOUS SHOCK
(1) Definite illness
(2) Actionable if:
(a) accompanying physical injury
(b) plaintiff feared such injury *(Dulieu v. White (1902))*
(3) Near relative within 'disaster area': *(Hinz v. Berry (1971)*
(Hambrook v. Stokes (1925))
(4) Rescuers — *(Chadwick v. BRB (1967))*
(5) Aftermath cases:
(Boardman v. Saunderson (1961))
(McLoughlin v. O'Brien (1982))

TYPE OF DAMAGE
Once a general rule — duty to avoid physical injury or damage to property

ECONOMIC LOSS

| NEGLIGENT STATEMENTS | NEGLIGENT ACTS |
| *Hedley v. Byrne* | *Junior Books* |

MULTIPLE CHOICE QUESTIONS

Choose the alternative which provides the best solution to the question or completes the sentence most satisfactorily.

1. In cases based on negligence:
    (a) the test of negligence is subjective
    (b) the plaintiff must show that the defendant owed him a duty of care
    (c) the onus is always upon the defendant to disprove negligence

2. The "landmark" case of Hedley Byrne v Heller & Partners (1963) is particularly important to:
    (a) professional advisers
    (b) manufacturers
    (c) supermarkets

3. The following cases all concerned nervous shock, except:
    (a) Hinz v Berry (1970)
    (b) Boardman v Sanderson (1964)
    (c) Muirhead v Industrial Tank Specialities Ltd. & Ors. (1985)

4. In Spartan Steel & Alloys v Martin & Co. (Contractors) Ltd. (1972) which of the following claims was not admitted:
    (a) £368 for metal being processed
    (b) £400 — profit lost on that metal
    (c) £1767 that would have been made on further production but for the interruption

5. "Damages must not be too remote" — which is the correct test:
    (a) Directness
    (b) reasonable foreseeability
    (c) neither of the above

CHAPTER 3

NUISANCE

3.1 **Nuisance** has been defined as 'a wrong done to man by unlawfully disturbing him in the enjoyment of his property, or, in some cases, the exercise of a common right' (Sir Frederick Pollock). Nuisance may be public or private.

1. PUBLIC NUISANCE

3.2 Public nuisance is a crime, e.g. obstructing the highway. It is an act or omission which materially affects the reasonable comfort and convenience of a class of HM subjects and so, to some extent at least, is 'widespread and indiscriminate in its effects'. If many road users are inconvenienced by an unlawful obstruction, the law avoids a multiplicity of actions by prescribing a single prosecution leading to the punishment of the offender. Public nuisance, however, becomes actionable as a tort when:

(a) the plaintiff suffers **particular injury**, i.e. damage greater than that suffered by the public at large.

(b) the injury is direct and substantial.

3.3 **Particular injury** may include:

(i) *Bodily injury.* A taxi driver was struck in the eye by a golf ball. A golf hole was so near to the road as to be a public nuisance. *(Castle v. St. Augustine's Links (1922).)* To be a public nuisance the injury must have occurred on the highway not, say, a shop forecourt. *(Jacobs v. L.C.C. (1950).)*

(ii) *Damage to property.* Oily smuts from a refinery damaged paintwork on the plaintiff's car parked in the road. *(Halsey v. Esso (1961).)*

(iii) *Injury to economic interests* such as:

    (a) Extra expense. The obstruction of a navigable river caused the costly switching of goods from a barge to land transport. *(Rose v. Mills (1815).)*

    (b) Loss of trade. A doctor with a high income was delayed at a level crossing. *(Boyd v. G.N.R. (1895).)* In *Campbell v. Paddington Corporation (1911),* a grandstand, erected to view a procession, prevented C from letting her windows for the same purpose. In *Wilkes v. Hungerford Market Co. (1835)* the defendant's obstruction prevented access to a bookseller's premises. In all cases the loss must be substantial and peculiar to the plaintiff.

17

3.4   **The standard of liability in public nuisance** is fairly confused as there are cases favouring strict liability while a line of other cases favours fault liability. It would appear that fault is a requirement in cases of danger on the highways — *(Dymond v. Pearce (1972)*. In *The Wagon Mound (2) (1967)* the defendants were held liable for public nuisance because fire on the plaintiff's ship was held to be the foreseeable consequence of the defendant's wrongful act. Foreseeability appears to be the key although two members of the Court of Appeal in Dymond's case thought that rare cases could arise (e.g. supervening fog and unexplained rear light failure) where the nuisance caused unforeseeable damage so the possibility of public nuisance as a strict tort remains in theory at least.

In the context of defective premises the leading case of *Wringe v. Cohen (1940)* seems to have laid down a special strict liability applying only when dangers on (or over) the highway arise from want of repair (see Winfield & Jolowicz, p. 422).

One clear distinction between negligence and public nuisance remains. Regarding the latter and dangers on the highway, the duty is non-delegable whereas in negligence the occupier is not liable for the acts of an independent contractor.

2.   PRIVATE NUISANCE — A MATTER OF 'GIVE AND TAKE'

3.5   **Private nuisance** is unlawful interference with a person's use and enjoyment of land arising indirectly from an activity carried on by a neighbour. The essence is 'so use your land as not to injure your neighbour's'. It balances the right of a person to do what he wants on his own land against the right of his neighbour not to be disturbed.

3.6   **Intangible invasions.** Interests in land are protected against 'intangible invasions' such as noise, smoke, smell and vibration. Some interferences have to be tolerated but they become unlawful when they become unreasonable.

3.7   The word 'unreasonable' is not necessarily used in the same sense as in negligence which focuses on the conduct of the defendant; concern is instead upon the reasonableness of the defendant's activity. Carelessness may be a factor in 'unreasonableness' but no more; conversely a man's activity, despite his reasonable care, may nonetheless unlawfully disturb his neighbour.

3.8   **Factors determining reasonableness**
A number of factors, set out below with the initial letter in each case contributing the mnemonic LUCAS (well-known for shedding light!) help to determine whether a private nuisance arises in particular cases:

(a)   **Locality** will be relevant where the damage is 'interference with beneficial use' ('what is a nuisance in Belgravia may not be a nuisance in Bermondsey'). Locality is not relevant when the damage is physical.

(b) **Unreasonable and substantial** — the damage must be in these terms. It is measured against the rights of the plaintiff who must show that the interference exceeds what a reasonable occupier should have to endure. Conflicting interests have to be balanced in the matters of the conduct of the defendant and effect on the plaintiff. Negligence, on the other hand, concentrates on the conduct of the defendant and compares it to duty.

(c) **Conduct of the defendant** — any interference prompted by malice or spite is unlawful and therefore a nuisance. In *Christie v. Davey (1893)*, D beat trays against a party wall whenever C gave music lessons. Conduct may be unreasonable (but see 3.6) when reasonable care is not taken to prevent the interference, e.g. if, say, smells could be eliminated for a trifling expense, subsequent 'invasions' are likely to be held unreasonable.

(d) **Abnormal sensitivity** — sometimes the problem resides, not with the defendant, but with the excessive demands of a plaintiff seeking protection greater than generally required. Such a plaintiff is not permitted to restrict the reasonable activities of others. In *Robinson v. Kilvert (1889)* heat rose from a flat to damage sensitive brown paper manufactured by the defendant. The heat was not so excessive that it would have damaged paper generally. A plaintiff in such circumstances must protect his own property rather than restrict his neighbour.

(e) **Seriousness of the interference** — temporary disturbances may be justified but the defendant must not abuse his position *(Andrae v. Selfridge (1938))*. Interference must not be 'according to elegant and dainty modes . . . but according to the plain and sober . . . notions among the English'. Duration of the interference may be relevant in conjunction with other matters. Often nuisance arises from a **state of affairs** as continuing interferences are more likely to be unreasonable than single occurrences, especially where the complaint is of interference with 'beneficial use'. An escape of fire was held a nuisance in *Spicer v. Smee (1946)* when a bungalow was destroyed through defective wiring in the adjoining property. This isolated event can be reconciled with 'continuity of wrong', the gist of nuisance, by regarding the keeping of a dangerous property as a 'state of affairs'. In fact all wrongful escapes are capable of being nuisances but each case depends on its own facts.

EXHIBIT 3

PRIVATE NUISANCE

INTERFERENCE

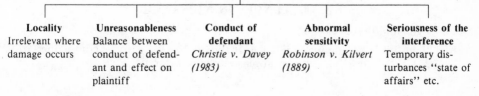

Locality	Unreasonableness	Conduct of defendant	Abnormal sensitivity	Seriousness of the interference
Irrelevant where damage occurs	Balance between conduct of defendant and effect on plaintiff	*Christie v. Davey (1983)*	*Robinson v. Kilvert (1889)*	Temporary disturbances "state of affairs" etc.

19

3.9   **What damage is actionable?** Nuisance is not actionable per se. The plaintiff must prove:

(a)   Interference with beneficial use (e.g. enjoyment of land). The relevance of locality is noted above as is the standard in terms of 'plain and sober and simple notions', or

(b)   Damage to property and premises. In this case locality is irrelevant. In *St. Helen's Smelting v. Tipping (1865)* the industrial character of the locality did not save the defendant when fumes from the smelting works damaged trees and shrubs.

The position in regard to bodily injury is not clear. As private nuisance protects interests in property, the view has been expressed that no action lies in nuisance for personal injury. Salmond, however, suggests that all the plaintiff's reasonably foreseeable loss is recoverable *(Howard Electric Ltd. v. Mooney Ltd. (1974))*.

3.10   **Who can sue in private nuisance?** The occupier can sue but tenants under notice (or at will) suffer certain restrictions and may not secure injunctions. A reversioner can sue for permanent injury to his property. A person who has use of land without possession or proprietary interests, cannue sue *(Malone v. Laskey (1907))*.

3.11   **Who can be sued in private nuisance?**

(a)   The occupier is liable for all nuisances on his premises during his occupancy on the basis that he has 'management and control'. This makes him liable for nuisances created by servants, contractors, licensees etc. He is not liable for the acts of trespassers or unauthorised acts, unless he knowingly allows them to continue.

(b)   Non-occupiers who may be liable:

    (i)   the creator of the nuisance by misfeance even when not in occupation.

    (ii)   the landlord who authorises his tenant to create or continue a nuisance *(Harris v. James (1876))*.

    (iii)   the landlord who lets premises with a nuisance on them — no contract between the landlord and tenant will defeat the claim against the landlord who knows of the nuisance.

    (iv)   the landlord may be liable for a breach of repair obligations. Also failure to repair, when S.8, 11/12 Landlord & Tenant Act 1985 apply, makes a landlord liable.

3.   DEFENCES IN NUISANCE

3.12   **Effectual defences**

(a)   **Rebuttal** is an adequate defence. It shows that the activity complained of is not a nuisance, i.e. not an unreasonable interference.

(b) **Specific agreement** may amount to authorising of the nuisance by the plaintiff, but the defence failed in *Pwllback Colliery Co. Ltd. v. Woodman (1915)* when coal dust deposited on 'other' land of the defendant's landlord was not a necessary outcome of trade and was not expressly authorised in the lease between the parties.

(c) **Prescription.** A private nuisance is legalised after 20 years but time runs from the plaintiff's awareness of it. In *Sturges v. Bridgman (1897)* the defendant's noise and vibration ran for more than twenty years but it was not the cause of a complaint until the defendant's neighbour, a doctor, built a consulting room adjacent to the site of the noisy operations. An injunction was granted as the activity was not a nuisance until the consulting room was built. A defendant must not abuse his prescriptive right *(Shoreham U.D.C. v. Dolphin Canadian Proteins Ltd. (1972))*.

(d) **Statutory authority.** Activities that would be a nuisance may be sanctioned by statute but if the defendant's conduct exceeds that allowed by the statute the defence will fail.

(e) **Other defences** include: contributory negligence; inevitable accident; act of stranger and probably Act of God.

3.13 Ineffectual defences

(a) **Public benefit** does not avail the defendant. No consideration of public utility can be suffered to deprive an individual of his legal rights without compensation *(Adams v. Ursell (1913))*.

(b) **Care and skill.** It is no defence that all possible care and skill are used to prevent the operation complained of becoming a nuisance.

(c) **Volenti non fit injuria.** It is no defence that the plaintiff came to the nuisance.

(d) **Reasonable use of property.** A person causing a nuisance cannot claim that he is making reasonable use of the property. No use is reasonable if it causes substantial discomfort to others or is a danger to their property.

(e) **Contributory acts of others.** It is no defence that the defendant's act would not amount to nuisance unless others acting independently of him did the same thing at the same time. In *Pride of Derby etc. Angling Assn. v. British Celanese Ltd. (1953)* a number of defendants polluted the plaintiff's fishery. They were jointly and severally liable.

4. INSURANCE ASPECTS OF NUISANCE

3.14 There are clear liability insurance implications for:

(a) Householders. e.g. A fire caused by a visitor could spread to neighbouring premises. Also following *Wringe v. Cohen* liability can arise through dangers created on the highway through lack of repair.

(b) Landlords. Absentee landlords may be liable *(Heap v. Ind Coope & Allsop Ltd. (1940))*.

(c)   Builders may be liable as creators of nuisances (e.g. interference with some form of servitude). Also, unfenced excavations near the highway may create danger rendering them liable.

(d)   Manufacturers may be liable for activities on their premises interfering with others. e.g. Smells, vibration and other matters leading to pollution.

(e)   Vehicle users are capable of creating road obstructions.

A liability policy covering only liability for negligence is insufficient in every case. Nuisance can succeed where negligence fails although in the case of public nuisance it seems that some form of fault is required in most cases (see 3.4 above).

CHAPTER 4

TRESPASS AND DEFAMATION

1. TRESPASS

4.1 Trespass has three forms:

(a) **Trespass to the person.** This includes assault; battery and false imprisonment.

    (i) **Trespass and negligence.** Trespass to the person can be intentional or unintentional. In all cases of the latter the plaintiff had to prove that the defendant was negligent and this was approved by the Court of Appeal in *Letang v. Cooper (1965)* when the defendant's car ran over the plaintiff who was sunbathing near parked cars. Trespass to the person is now effectively limited to cases where the defendant's conduct has been intentional.

    (ii) **Defences to trespass to the person.**
        (a) Legal justification, e.g. lawful arrest.
        (b) Consent of the plaintiff.
        (c) Defence of property and self-defence related to assault and battery provided excessive force is not used.
        (d) Reasonable chastisement e.g. parents, teachers who reasonably believe it to be necessary to preserve order.
        (e) Statutory power.
        (f) Contributory negligence.
        (g) Inevitable accident — In *Stanley v. Powell (1891)* the plaintiff was struck by a pellet which deflected off a tree even though the gun had been properly handled by the defendant.

(b) **Trespass to land.** This occurs when there is a direct invasion of land in the possession of the plaintiff. A defendant who, having entered lawfully, remains when unauthorised to do so, is guilty of trespass. Defences include: Legal justification/authority (e.g. entry by the police, entry under National Parks and Countryside Act 1949, entry to abate a nuisance); consent; irrevocable licence; repossession of property.

(c) **Trespass to goods.** The complex law relating to interference with goods led to the Torts (Interference with Goods) Act 1977 which introduced the collective term 'wrongful interference with goods' to cover conversion, trespass to goods, negligence and any other torts resulting in damage to goods or an interest therein. The distinctions between conversion and trespass to goods remain.

(i) **Conversion** is the intentional dealing in goods which is seriously inconsistent with the possession or right to immediate possession of another person. It protects 'control' rather than physical condition of goods. Conversion is one of the most difficult areas of the law of tort and for the reader requiring further information Street on Torts (Seventh Edition, pages 29 to 52) is recommended but it should be remembered that detailed information is not likely to be required for the C.I.I. examination.

(ii) **Trespass to goods.** This involves an intentional or negligent interference with goods in the possession of the plaintiff provided the interference is direct. The tort protects the plaintiff's interest in the retention of goods. It also protects his interest in the physical condition of the goods as well as his interest in the inviolability of his goods.

4.2   **Remedies** for the torts described include:

(a)   damages;

(b)   an order for restitution or damages in lieu.

2.   DEFAMATION

4.3   Defamation involves injury to a person's feelings after interference with his reputation. It is the publication of a statement which 'tends to lower the plaintiff in the estimation of right-thinking people'.

4.4   **Two forms of defamation.** One form is spoken words (slander) and the other is written words (libel). See below:

Libel	Slander
(a) permanent form	non-permanent
(b) actionable per se	actionable on proof of special damage
(c) sometimes a crime	never a crime

(Libel may occur in films *(Yousoupoff v. MGM (1934))* and, by the Defamation Act 1934, the broadcasting of words is treated as being permanent.)

4.5   **Essentials of defamation**
To succeed the plaintiff must show that the statement:

(a)   was published.

(b)   was defamatory.

(c)   referred to the plaintiff.

(c)   caused special damage.

The test for defamation is based not on the intention but the 'meaning which would be imputed by reasonable people'. Not only is the author exposed to this risk but so too are the printers, publishers and negligent distributors.

4.6 **Innuendo** can be defamatory. In *Tolley v. Fry (1931)* an advertisement implied that a famous golfer had compromised his amateur status by permitting the use of his name. The golfer knew nothing of the advertisement until publication.

4.7 **Defamation is of identifiable inviduals** — 'all brokers are crooks' is not actionable by a single broker.

4.8 **Defences to defamation**

(a) Unintentional defamation (Sec. 4, Defamation Act 1952). The defendant can make an 'offer of amends', which, if accepted and performed, ends the matter.

(b) Justification. Truth is a complete defence but 'spent convictions' (Rehabilitation of Offenders Act 1974) must not be maliciously published.

(c) Fair comment. Honest statements on matters of public interest are permitted but must be comment only and not prompted by malice. This defence is important to the press.

(d) Privilege is a defence that facilitates communications between people without inviting actions for defamation. Examples:

    (i) Absolute privilege (Parliament and government).

    (ii) Judicial proceedings covers statements by judges, advocates, jurors, witnesses or parties in the course of proceedings about those proceedings.

    (iii) Qualified privilege may be claimed by a defendant when under a duty to communicate to persons interested in receiving it (e.g. a reference).

4.9 **Damages**
Damages are the main remedy but an injunction may be appropriate to prevent the publication of defamatory material.

EXHIBIT 4

RYLANDS v. FLETCHER

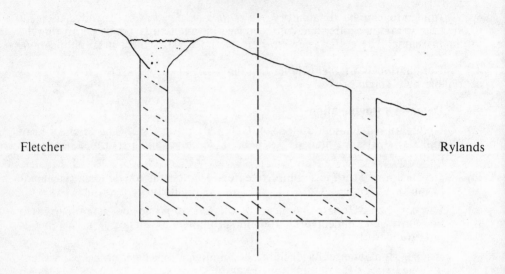

Fletcher   Rylands

LIMITS OF THE RULE

(i) Escape of ''mischievous thing''
(ii) Non-natural use of land.

CHAPTER 5

STRICT LIABILITY

5.1   **Strict liability** describes liability that does not depend upon proof of fault. The term supersedes 'absolute liability' which refers to situations in which there is virtually no defence. This chapter focuses upon particular cases of strict liability, viz: *Rylands v. Fletcher; Fire; and Animals.* Breach of statutory duty and liability for defective goods are covered elsewhere.

1.   *RYLANDS v. FLETCHER (1868)*

5.2   **The facts.** A landowner (F) engaged independent contractors to construct a reservoir on his land on which there was a filled-in mine shaft that communicated with the plaintiff's (R's) working mine. The contractors overlooked the shaft and, when the reservoir was filled, water penetrated the shaft and flooded R's mine (see Exhibit 4). The usual causes of action of the day were not available to R but the defendant was held liable on a general principle of strict liability. The defendant was held liable as the occupier of land for the damage caused by the escape of 'mischievous things' from that land. The House of Lords upheld the judgment but added a requirement, now an established part of the rule, that the defendant's use of land was 'non-natural'.

5.3   **The Rule.** The rule is 'A person who for his own purposes brings on his land . . . and keeps there anything likely to do damage if it escapes, must keep it at his peril and . . . is answerable for all damage which is the natural consequence of the escape even if . . . guilty of no negligence'.

5.4   **The elements of liability in *Rylands v. Fletcher***

(a)   The defendant must be an occupier or an owner controlling things on land.

(b)   Things must be **brought and kept on the land**. The rule does not apply to land or things naturally on it, e.g. noxious weeds, vermin, or water. In *Giles v. Walker (1890)* there was no liability when the defendant ploughed up the land causing thistle on the adjoining land. But liability arises for the escape of natural things that are artificially accumulated, e.g. rain-water in a man-made lake. Also there is liability for causing the escape of natural things, e.g. creating an aperture in an artificial embankment (e.g. *Whalley v. Lancashire & Yorkshire Railway (1884)*) to relieve pressure as water built up. However, the removal of an embankment or artificial structure which protected the land against the natural flow of water does not of itself create liability under the rule. There is no liability for the prevention of flood water coming on to land when it is diverted to neighbouring land.

(c)   There must be **escape** from the defendant's land. Damage wholly within the land is not within the rule *(Read v. Lyons (1947))*.

(d)   Things **likely to do mischief** if they escape — this depends on the facts of the case.

(e)   The use of land must be **non-natural**. This is 'special use bringing with it increased danger to others, and must not merely be the ordinary use of the land or use which is proper for the general benefit of the community' *(Rickards v. Lothian (1913))*. Ordinary use goes beyond domestic or agricultural use and may include the working of a mine; the wiring of premises for electricity. The storage in bulk of water, gas, and electricity have been held to be examples of non-natural user. In *British Celanese v. Hunt (1969)* storing strips of metal foil in the manufacture of electrical components was held to be a natural use in view of public benefit from the activity. The non-natural user requirement means that Rylands v. Fletcher will only apply in the most exceptional circumstances but it remains a flexible tool enabling the courts to take acount of contemporaneous needs. Given that Rylands v. Fletcher virtually makes the occupier an insurer of accidental harm caused by the risk he created, the requirement enables the court to identify circumstances when application of the rule is unreasonable.

5.5   **Who can sue and for what damage?**
Successful actions under the rule have been brought by the occupiers of land and non-occupiers although the rights of the latter have been doubted. These doubts have their origin in the belief that Rylands v. Fletcher is analogous with nuisance seeking only to protect interests in land. Most authorities, however, support the view that the plaintiff does not have to be the occupier of adjoining land. As to the type of damage, the greatest difficulties concern personal injuries but it is generally accepted that the occupier will have a right of claim *(Hale v. Jennings Bros. (1938))*. Non-occupiers have succeeded in personal injury claims *(Shiffman v. Order of St. John (1936))* but the doubt can only finally be resolved by the House of Lords.

The rule does not protect pure financial loss for either occupier or non-occupier and, unlike private nuisance, there appears to be no protection for mere interference with the plaintiff's enjoyment of his land.

5.6   **Defences to *Rylands v. Fletcher***

(a)   **Consent.** The tenant may have consented to the 'thing' being brought on to the defendant's land. A tenant, for example, is deemed to consent to anything kept by the landlord on his premises at the time of taking the lease. The plaintiff in *Peters v. Prince of Wales Theatre (1943)* failed following flooding from a sprinkler leakage system installed to prevent fire. Also occupants of different parts of the same building may have consented to certain risks. The occupants of a lower floor may suffer damage from water falling from an upper floor as the water, whether collected from the roof or carried in pipes, will have been collected for mutual benefit *(Rickards v. Lothian (1913))*. Liability, however, may still arise in negligence.

(b)   **Default of the plaintiff.** The plaintiff may be a trespasser or one who invites danger. Also, as in nuisance, the problem may reside in the abnormal sensitivity of the plaintiff's property and not the escape.

(c)　**Act of God.** This arises where the accident or injury could not have been avoided by human care or foresight and in which there was no human intervention. In *Nichols v. Marsland (1876)* the defendant created artificial lakes by damming a stream. Construction was sound and adequate as far as could be foreseen but a storm of exceptional severity caused flooding on the plaintiff's land.

(d)　**Act of a stranger.** The important elements are:

(i)　There is no control over strangers and therefore no liability, e.g. *Richards v. Lothian (1913)* a malicious person turned on a tap causing a flood. In *Box v. Jubb (1879)* a stranger emptied his reservoir into the defendant's reservoir which then overflowed into the plaintiff's land; no liability attached.

(ii)　It is for the defendant to show that the escape was the deliberate or conscious act of a stranger over whom he had no control and against whose acts he could not reasonably be expected to take precautions.

(iii)　The occupier may be liable if negligent in the matter of precautionary steps.

(iv)　Trespassers are strangers but servants and authorised contractors are not. It is generally difficult for the occupier to distance himself from the activities of family, guests or persons authorised to be on his land.

(e)　**Statutory authority.** Two cases emerge: (i) statutes imposing duties; (ii) statues 'permitting' activities.

(i)　Statutes imposing duties enable the defendant acting in pursuance of the duties to avoid liability under the rule but liability may arise under negligence. In *Green v. Chelsea Waterworks (1854)* a burst water main flooded the plaintiff's premises. There was no liability as the company had a duty to maintain a continuous water supply and had not been negligent.

(ii)　Statutes permitting activities sometimes impose strict liability for the escape of dangerous things (e.g. Nuclear Installations Acts 1965 and 1969) but more often there is silence on the rule in Rylands v. Fletcher. In such statutes liability arises if there is an escape *(Charing Cross Electricity Supply v. Hydraulic Power Co. (1914))*.

2.　LIABILITY FOR FIRE

5.7　Liability for fire may arise under negligence, nuisance, or under Rylands v. Fletcher when the relevant conditions apply.

5.8　**The Fire Prevention (Metropolis Act) 1774, S. 86** shows that it was felt that liability should be fault-based. S. 86 provides that an occupier on whose land a fire 'accidentally begins' is not liable for the resultant damage. An accidental fire was defined in *Filliter v. Phippard (1847)* as 'fire produced by mere chance or incapable of being traced to any particular cause'. Thus, when traced to negligence, nuisance, or a Rylands v. Fletcher object, the defence of S. 86 will not apply.

5.9   **Negligence.** This is not protected by S. 86 and even if a fire is 'accidentally caused', there will be liability if it spreads through negligence. Unless there is negligence there is no liability for an ordinary domestic fire which spreads *(Sochacki v. Sas (1947))*. Res ipsa loquitur does not apply in these circumstances even though the fire is deliberately lit. The occupier is liable for the negligence of servants and independent contractors, the latter on the grounds that fire is hazardous. In *H & N Emmanuel V. GLC (1971)*, a contractor engaged to do demolition started a fire that spread through his negligence. The GLC was liable under the principle in *Beaulieu v. Finglam (1401)* as they had right of control.

5.10   **Strict liability.** This arises if Rylands v. Fletcher applies. In *Musgrove v. Pandelis (1919)* petrol in a car was regarded as a Rylands object although a different view would be taken today. The best guide is *Mason v. Levy Auto Parts of England Ltd. (1967)* in which the escape was of fire from the objects and not of the objects themselves. The defendant was held liable for (a) having brought inflammable things to his land and keeping them in such a way that if they caught fire, it was likely that the fire would spread; (b) having done this in the course of 'non-natural' use of land; and (c) the object having caught fire and the spread of that fire. The defendant had kept wooden stacking cases in oily conditions. Liability for fire under Rylands v. Fletcher is founded upon 'occupation and control' making the defendant liable for the acts of servants, visitors and independent contractors *(H & N Emmanuel v. GLC (1971)*. There is no strict liability for an Act of God or the act of a stranger.

5.11   **Private nuisance.** This too may involve strict liability unprotected by S. 86. An example is *Spicer v. Smee (1946)*, a fire case based on nuisance.

3.   LIABILITY FOR ANIMALS

5.12   Liability for animals has 'travelled in a compartment of its own' culminating in the Animals Act 1971 but liability may still arise under negligence or nuisance. It is useful to start with the common law liability which arose under three headings: (a) scienter; (b) cattle trespass; (c) liability for dogs.

COMMON LAW LIABILITY

5.13   **Scienter liability** arose under the 'risk principle', i.e. a person responsible for creating a potentially hazardous situation should be liable for damage ensuing from the risk. A person who kept an animal fierce by nature (ferae naturae), e.g. a tiger, was strictly liable for injuries the animal caused. It was a matter of law as to which species were 'fierce by nature'. It was immaterial that a particular animal was more or less tamed. The owner was presumed to know (scienter) of the nature of the animal and the risk created. In the case of animals tame by nature (mansuetae naturae) strict liability only arose if the keeper knew (or ought to have known) of any dangerous propensities. The expression 'every dog is entitled to its first bite' is well-known. In such cases the plaintiff had to prove scienter, i.e. the defendant had knowledge of these dangerous propensities. Once the keeper was fixed with that knowledge he thereafter acquiesced to a hazardous situation.

5.14 **Cattle trespass.** The salient points of the common law position:

(a) A person whose cattle entered the plaintiff's land was strictly liable for the damage caused.

(b) Liability was not limited to land but extended to personal injuries.

(c) cattle trespass was actionable per se.

(d) It was a defence that the animal escaped from the highway (although liability could still arise in negligence).

Strict liability has been a convenient and inexpensive device for the adjusting relevant issues that commonly concern members of the agricultural community in which some 'give and take' in such matters is expected. Cattle has been defined as — bulls, cows, sheep, goats, pigs, horses, asses, and poultry.

]5.15 **Liability for dogs.** This could arise under 'scienter' but the Dogs Act 1906 made liability strict where dogs attacked farm animals.

LIABILITY UNDER THE ANIMALS ACT 1971

5.16 Strict liability is retained for two categories which are now: (a) all animals of a dangerous species; (b) any animal of a non-dangerous species that has shown 'abnormal characteristics'.

5.17 (a) **Dangerous species**
The definition in Section 6 is of an animal:

(i) not commonly domesticated in the British Isles.

(ii) which, when fully grown normally has such characteristics that it is likely, unless restrained, to cause severe damage or that any damage it may cause is 'likely to be severe'.

It is a question of law whether a species belongs to this category. The characteristics of the individual animal remain irrelevant. Animals dangerous to property only may be of a 'dangerous species'.

The liability is strict. Section 2(1) provides 'where any damage is caused . . . the keeper is liable except as provided by the Act'. The test appears to be that of directness and not foreseeability.

5.18 (b) **Non-dangerous species**
Section 2(2) requires the plaintiff to show that (i) the animal had certain abnormal characteristics and (ii) that the keeper knew of these characteristics. The damage, again described in terms of 'likely to be severe', must flow from the animal's known dangerous characteristics.

5.19 **Who is liable?**
According to the Act the keeper is liable. The keeper is the person who owns the animal or has it in his possession. Also it will be the head of the household if a person under 16 is the owner or person who possesses the animal.

31

5.20   Liability for dogs

Section 3 of the Act replaces the Dogs Acts 1906/1928 and liability for killing or injuring livestock remains strict but certain defences are available under Section 5. Section 9 on the other hand provides a defence for the killing of a dog which worries livestock.

5.21   Defences to actions under Sections 2 and 3

Section 5 provides defences in sub-sections as follows:

(1)   The plaintiff was wholly at fault (Sections 10 and 11 facilitate apportionment where the plaintiff was partly at fault).

(2)   The plaintiff voluntarily accepted the risk, e.g. intervening in a dog fight.

(3)   The plaintiff was a trespasser provided it is proved that the animal was not kept for protection. If the animal was kept for protection, the defendant must show that his keeping of the animal for that purpose was not unreasonable. In *Cummings v. Grainger (1976)* a savage dog in a built-up area to protect scrap metal was not unreasonable. The plaintiff followed her friend who had gone to collect a car from the scrapyard. The friend was a licensee and the plaintiff a trespasser. In regard to (2) above she had willingly accepted the risk and in regard to (3)(b) the keeping of the dog was not unreasonable. Her claim failed. The Guard Dogs Act 1975 now makes it a crime to allow a guard dog to roam freely on premises unless under the control of a handler. This Act does not create any civil liability but a breach might deprive a keeper of the defence under S. 5(3)(b) keeping an animal for reasonable protection, but it would not defeat the defence of volenti (S.5(2)).

5.22   Cattle trespass

Section 4 of the Act imposes a modern form of strict liability on a person in possession of livestock where:

(a)   damage is done to the land or to any property on it which is in the possession of the other person;

(b)   any expenses are reasonably incurred by that other person in keeping the livestock while it cannot be restored to the person who possesses it or while detained in pursuance to Section 7.

Cattle trespass is no longer actionable per se and similarly no strict liability arises for damage to goods of a person not in the occupation of land or for personal injuries regardless of the status of the plaintiff.

5.23   Defences to cattle trespass

(a)   Where the plaintiff is wholly at fault.

(b)   Contributory negligence.

(c)   Straying from the highway where the livestock was lawfully on the highway, but a duty of care attaches to any person who takes animals on to the highway.

(d)   Breach of duty to fence. If the straying would not have occurred but for a breach of such a duty a defence arises even though the duty may not have been owed to the defendant. There is no general duty to fence to keep livestock out but the duty may come from contract, custom, easement or statute.

5.24   Straying on to the highway

Section 8(1) of the 1971 Act abolished the common law rule (the rule in *Searle v. Wallbank (1947)*) that there was no duty to prevent animals from straying from land on to the highway. Liability is now determined by the ordinary rules of negligence *(Hoskin v. Rodgers (1982))*. The duty is in respect of non-dangerous animals generally. However, by Section 8(2) a breach of duty is not committed by reason only of the placing of an animal on common land provided tht the person concerned had a right to place the animal on that land. In *Davies v. Davies (1974)*, the plaintiff's car struck sheep that had strayed from registered common land. He failed to recover for the damage to his car.

5.25   Liability in Negligence and Nuisance

(a)   In *negligence* the ordinary rules apply. Thus,

   (i)   the type of harm must be reasonably foreseeable. *Draper v. Hodder (1972)* — injury to a child resulted when Jack Russell terriers had been assembled in a pack, a state in which they were known to be aggressive. Injury by bowling over or scratching was foreseeable. It was no defence that biting was not foreseeable.

   (ii) negligence may arise from failure to control *(Gomberg v. Smith (1962))*. The defendant had brought his dog to the highway and had a duty to control it.

   (iii) Liability in negligence is limited to the harm associated with the animal's nature. The defendant is not liable simply because the animal acts out of character.

5.26   **Nuisance** may be resorted to by the plaintiff when there is no strict liability, cattle trespass or negligence. Large numbers of animals obstructing the highway may be a nuisance. Nuisance may also interfere with 'beneficial use', e.g. stench of pigs, cocks crowing for six weeks in a residential area.

MULTIPLE CHOICE QUESTIONS

Choose the alternative which provides the best answer or completes the sentence most satisfactorily.

1. Liability for fine:
    (a)   does not arise in the event of accidental negligence;
    (b)   is strict under the Fire Prevention (Metropolis) Act 1974;
    (c)   may arise through negligence, nuisance or Rylands v Fletcher.

2. Which of the following is not a Rylands v Fletcher defence?
    (a)   Act of God;
    (b)   Exercise of reasonable care;
    (c)   Consent of the plaintiff.

3. A dog strays on to neighbouring land and mutilates ducks. The keeper:
    (a)   is strictly liable;
    (b)   only liable if it has happened before;
    (c)   liable only if negligence can be proved.

4. A pet monkey, released from a cage by a mischievous boy, bites the plaintiff:
    (a)   the defendant is not liable — "act of stranger";
    (b)   the defendant is strictly liable;
    (c)   the defendant is not liable as the monkey was not wild.

5. A bull-dog enters Smith's garden attacking Smith, his turkey and pet rabbit. The keeper is liable without proof of negligence, or knowledge of "abnormal characteristics" for injury to:
    (a)   Smith;
    (b)   the rabbit;
    (c)   the turkey.

CHAPTER 6

LIABILITY OF EMPLOYERS TO EMPLOYEES

6.1   An employer is not an insurer of his employees. Liability for injuries arises only when, outside special contract provisions, there has been a breach of duty at common law or under statute.

1.   EMPLOYERS' COMMON LAW DUTY

6.2   The employer has a duty to take reasonable care of his staff. The duty is personal, non-delegable and, although general in nature, is conveniently considered under four heads of liability.

6.3   **The duty to take reasonable care to provide:**

(a)   **a safe place of work.** Reasonable steps must be taken to make the premises safe *(Latimer v. A.E.C. (1953))*. The duty applies also to means of access and is not necessarily discharged by giving a warning. The duty extends to third party premises where employees are working but the requirements vary with the circumstances but sometimes the issue is approached from a different standpoint, i.e. the duty relating to a safe system of work (see (c) below).

(b)   **adequate plant etc.** Reasonable care and skill should be taken to provide and maintain adequate plant and machinery. The employer may fail, for want of care, to provide necessary equipment or suitable equipment, or, having provided it, may not maintain it. At common law the employer who had acquired equipment from a reputable supplier was not liable for injury caused by a latent defect in such equipment. In *Davie v. New Merton Board Mills (1959)* the plaintiff suffered an eye injury when a tool which had a latent defect splintered. The employer was not liable. The problem in such cases occurs when the plaintiff is unable to identify the manufacturer whose negligence may have created the defect. The *Employers Liability (Defective Equipment) Act 1969* remedies the position by making an employer liable for injury caused by equipment supplied by him even though the fault is wholly or partly that of a third party whether identified or not.

(c)   **Safe system of work.** This, broadly, is 'the distinction between what is permanent or continuous on the one hand, and what is merely casual and emerges in the day's work on the other'. It includes physical layout, the sequence of the work, the provision of warnings and notices, the issue of special instructions, and modifications that become necessary as the work proceeds. Each case, as in other aspects of the duty, turns on its own facts. An employer assists his case, but not necessarily conclusively, when he has followed the usual and approved practice of the trade. The system should take account of the defects of particular workmen, e.g. *Paris v. Stepney B.C. (1951)*, the case of the 'one-eyed welder'. In contrast, an employer is entitled to expect workmen to take reasonable care of themselves in a manner commensurate with their skill and experience and the danger inherent in the work. The rights of a workman on third party's premises will be based on occupier's liability, but as against the employer the matter often becomes that of the 'system of work'. In *General Cleaning Contractors v. Christmas (1953)*, a window cleaner had not been provided with wedges nor given instructions when the absence of hooks prevented the use of safety belts. The employer, it was held, had not taken reasonable care to provide a safe system of work.

(d)   **Competent fellow servants.** Before 1948 an employer was not liable for injury to an employee carelessly caused by a fellow worker. The defence of 'common employment' prevented an employer from being held vicariously liable for the torts of one servant against another. However, a workman could sue, in appropriate circumstances, for breach of the personal duty of the employer to take reasonable care to provide competent fellow workers. In *Hudson v. Ridge Manufacturing (1957)*, a practical joker caused injury to the plaintiff. The joker had previously been reprimanded for horseplay. His continued employment put the employer in breach of duty. Now that the 'common employment' defence has been abolished, claims under this head will be rare and will be most likely to occur when the tort is not within the course of employment, which is important in the context of vicarious liability (see Chapter 7).

6.4   **The duty of care is not discharged by delegation.** The duty is personal and cannot be discharged by delegation. In *Wilsons & Clyde Coal Co. v. English (1938)*, a miner was leaving the pit when the haulage plant was put into operation and he was injured. The 'system' was unsafe and the company's contention that they had delegated responsibility to a competent official did not avail them in the context of a personal duty.

6.5   **Employee's duty to employer.** An employee must carry out the employment with reasonable care. This is implied by contract. When an employer is vicariously liable for injury to one employee by another, the employer is entitled to recover his loss from the employee causing the injury. The duty of the negligent employee to indemnify the employer is currently enacted in the Civil Liability (Contribution) Act 1978 dealing, as it does, with joint tortfeasors. In *Lister v. Romford Ice & Cold Storage Co. (1957)*, a father and son were fellow workers. The son injured the father who recovered damages from the employer. The latter successfully sought an indemnity from the son for his breach of contract. In fact this was an insurer exercising subrogation rights. Insurers have since agreed not to exercise subrogation rights in these circumstances as to do so would have serious repercussions on industrial relations.

2. EMPLOYERS' STATUTORY DUTIES

6.6   Some statutes (e.g. Guard Dogs Act 1975) expressly exclude a civil action for a breach of obligations arising. In others, but it is rare, it sets down that a breach is actionable in tort (Consumer Safety Act 1978). Where the statute is silent on this issue, the court has to discover the intention of Parliament and reference to decided cases becomes essential. In the field of industrial injury, it is the rule and not the exception that an admissible claim arises when injury results from an employer's failure to observe statutory obligations.

6.7   **Establishing civil liability.** Breach of statutory duty is a tort separate and distinct from negligence, but as with the latter, the onus of proof attaches to the plaintiff who must show that:

(a)   the statutory duty was owed to him.

(b)   the statute imposed a duty on the defendant;

(c)   the defendant was in breach;

(d)   the plaintiff suffered harm in consequence of the breach provided it was not too remote.

6.8   **Application to employment cases.** Legislation has been used to impose standards often stricter than negligence in the desire to protect bodily security. In fact the tort is often classed with the 'strict' torts as an action may lie even though the defendant's breach may not have been negligent or intentional. The Factories Act 1961, to be replaced by regulations under the Health & Safety at Work Act 1974, is the primary example of statutory duties attaching to employers.

6.9   **The Factories Act 1961** provides that:

(a)   **Dangerous machinery should be fenced.** All prime movers, transmission, and other dangerous machinery (i.e. capable of injuring a reasonably acting person) must be securely fenced unless equally safe by position or construction. Fencing must be of sound construction and kept in position when in motion or use. The duty is absolute in that it is no defence that fencing would make the machine unusable *(Summers v. Frost (1955))*. The duty is owed to every person employed or working on the premises and not merely the operator. The fence is intended to keep the worker out and not the machine or its product in. In *Nicholls v. Austin (1946)* there was no breach when a piece of wood flew out of the machine.

(b)   **Hoists and lifts** must be of good mechanical construction, sound materials, adequate strength, and properly maintained. This duty too is absolute; chains, ropes, and lifting tackle must also be of good construction; the obligation is of a continuing nature.

(c)   **Premises.** Floors, steps, stairs, passages, gangways, and ladders must be properly constructed and properly maintained. The duty is absolute but a floor is not necessarily in an inefficient condition because of some transient and exceptional condition *(Latimer v. A.E.C. (1953))*. Floors, passages, and stair shall, as far as is reasonably practicable, be kept free from any obstruction and from substances likely to cause people to slip. Also as far as is reasonably practicable, there must be provided and maintained safe means of access to any place of work, which should be made and kept safe.

The term 'reasonably practicable' is considered to be stricter than negligence and it is for the employer to prove that compliance was impracticable.

6.10   **Particular trades.** The Mines & Quarries Acts 1954 and 1969 contain stringent requirements for all kinds of mines and quarries. Ultimately these too will be replaced by regulations under the Health & Safety at Work Act 1974. The agriculture and construction industries are also subject to regulations.

CHAPTER 7

VICARIOUS LIABILITY

7.1   Vicarious liability. This form of liability is strict in one sense. It attaches to a party, not because he has committed a tort, but because of his relationship with the actual wrongdoer, e.g. a master is liable for the torts of his servant committed in the course of employment. This is the principal application of vicarious liability.

7.2   The rationale. The reasons for making an employer liable can be summarised:

(a)   It is more likely to satisfy the desire to find a financially responsible defendant.

(b)   It induces the employer to fix maximum safety standards.

7.3   The basis of vicarious liability. The plaintiff will succeed against the employer if he can show:

(a)   the existence of a master and servant relationship.

(b)   that the servant committed the tort in the course of employment.

1. MASTER & SERVANT

7.4   THE MASTER & SERVANT RELATIONSHIP. This relationship, under which there is a contract of service, has to be distinguished from that of principal and contractor (contract for services). Vicarious liability arises in the former case but not the latter. In making the distinction, certain tests (they are not principles of law) guide the courts: the control test; the integration test; the multiple test.

(a)   **The control test** is the traditional test and, under it, a person is a servant where the master retains control of the actual performance of the work. Thus, the master directs not only what to do but how to do it. However, control is not the only factor and, given the existence of highly skilled and/or professionally qualified employees, the test can be difficult to apply. A hospital authority would not be able to direct a brain surgeon in the performance of his work. Such skilled workers can clearly still be employees and it has been suggested that the test should be applied only to the incidental features of employment such as 'when and where' rather than 'how'.

(b)   **The integration test** has gained some approval. 'A person is a servant when his work is an integral part of the business, whereas under a contract for services, his work is not integrated into the business but is only an accessory to it'. e.g. a chauffeur is integrated in the business but a taxi-driver is an accessory to it. One works in the business, the other on his own account. In *Morren v. Swinton & Pendlebury U.D.C. (1965)* an engineer, though not subject to control in performing his work, was sufficiently 'integrated' to make the local authority liable for his tort.

39

(c)   **The multiple test** is complex and takes account of: control; ownership of tools; the allocation of financial risk by reference to chance of profit and risk of loss; the terms of the contract. In *Ready Mixed Concrete (South East) Ltd. v. Ministry of Social Security (1968)* the worker drove a ready mixed-concrete lorry bought on hire-purchase arranged with the company. The lorry had to carry the company's livery and it could not be used other than on company business. The driver had to maintain the lorry but the company could direct where it would be maintained. He also had to carry out the company's reasonable orders 'as though an employee'. Payment to the worker depended on the amount of concrete carried. The contract stated that the worker was not an employee but this could be overridden by the court if other factors indicated the contrary. McKenna J. applied a multiple test, holding that a contract of service arises: (i) where the servant agrees, for a wage of other remuneration, to provide his own work or skill in the performance of some service for his master; (ii) he agrees that in the performance of that service he will be subject to the other's control to a sufficient degree to make that other master; (iii) the other contract provisions are consistent with its being a contract of service. Despite the degree of control, it was held that the contract terms were consistent with a contract of carriage not of service. Some important conditions were inconsistent with a master-servant relationship, e.g. the driver had to make a vehicle with driver available at his own expense throughout the contract term and the chance of profit and risk of loss attached to him.

7.5   Some special cases:

(a)   **Hospital staffs** are servants, e.g. nurses, radiographers, surgeons, full or part-time. Surgeons and consultants are servants even though only employed on occasions. Only if the patient engages such a person privately will the hospital authority not be liable.

(b)   **Borrowed servants** — a strong presumption is that the general employer, who hires out or lends his servants, to a special employer, will be liable unless he can show that control has passed to the latter. Where a crane and driver were hired out, the general employer was responsible for the driver's negligence *(Mersey Docks & Harbour Board v. Coggins & Griffiths (1947))*.

7.6   **THE COURSE OF EMPLOYMENT.** A master is not liable unless the servant's tort is committed in the course of employment. To assist in the consideration of border-line cases, the following includes cases on either side of the border-line:

(a)   **Authorised act done in an authorised way.** The master will be liable.

(b)   **Authorised act done in an unauthorised way.** The master is liable as this is simply an improper mode of work. In *McKean v. Raynor Bros. (1942)*, a servant, instructed to deliver a message by lorry, took a car instead. The employer was liable for his negligent driving.

(c)   **Prohibited acts within the scope of employment** normally amount to improper ways of carrying out the work so making the employer liable. In *Limpus v. London General Omnibus Co. (1862)*, a driver, who had been warned not to race, raced with another bus and caused an accident. Held — employers liable. See also *Rose v. Plenty (1975)*, the case of the milkman and the thirteen year old boy.

(d)   **Prohibited acts outside the scope of employment.** In these cases the master will not be liable as the servant will not be carrying out the employment. In *Beard v. London General Omnibus Co. (1900)* a bus conductor, in the driver's absence, turned the bus round, thereby causing an accident. The employers were not liable.

7.7   **Criminal acts by the servant.** These have normally been committed for the servant's own benefit but, nonetheless, if committed in the course of employment, the employer will be liable. In *Lloyd v. Grace Smith & Co. (1912)*, a solicitor's conveyancing clerk fraudulently induced the plaintiff to transfer some property to him. He sold the property for personal profit. The defendant solicitors were liable as the clerk had the authority to do work of the kind that facilitated his fraud.

7.8   **Acts for own purposes.** Fraud (above) is such an act but other instances include:

(a)   **Frolics of their own.** In *Hilton v. Thos. Burton (Rhodes) Ltd. (1961)* demolition workers left the site in the employer's van to go to a cafe. The driver, an employee of the defendants, was negligent and killed the foreman. The employers were not liable as the men, not pursuing their employment, were on a 'frolic of their own'.

(b)   **Acts coincidental with duties.** The master is liable if the servant, while carrying out the work, does something for his own purposes and causes injury. In *Jefferson v. Derbyshire Farmers (1921)*, a servant lighted a cigarette while tapping a drum of benzol. The employers were liable for the spectacular outcome!

(c)   **Deviations.** If an employee goes on a journey for the employer but deviates from the route, it is a question of degree as to how far the deviation could be considered a separate route. In *Hemphill v. Williams (1966)*, Boys Brigade lads were being driven from Argyllsire to Glasgow. In defiance of instructions, the driver twice deviated from the intended route. An accident, for which the employers were held liable, occurred. The driver was primarily employed to drive to Glasgow and this he was still doing.

7.9   **A test for vicarious liability.** In all cases like the foregoing, to determine whether the servant was 'in the course of employment', the following question needs to be asked:

Was the servant performing a class of act he was employed to do, or, was he doing something he was not employed to do?

7.10 **Employees travelling to or from work.** When an employee, being driven to or from work, is injured by the negligent driving of a fellow worker, the employer will be vicariously liable only if the journey is in the course of employment. In *Vandyke v. Fender (1970)*, the injured employee was obliged to use the employer's vehicle and the 'obligation' brought his carriage as a passenger within the course of employment. In *Smith v. Stages & Anr. (1987)* The Court of Appeal modified the rule. Accordingly where travel home is from a place other than the normal base in the employee's own time and in his own car, notwithstanding the availability of alternative transport, then he is acting in the course of employment if the employer knows of and authorises the journey and, being entitled to order that travel should not take place on that particular day, failed to do so. (See Times Law Report, 2 December 1987.)

7.11 **Incidence of liability.** A workman remains personally liable for his own torts notwithstanding the master's vicarious liability. The latter is entitled to an indemnity or contribution from the servant unless he specifically ordered the tort or subsequently ratified it. The indemnity (see para. 6.5) is rarely sought.

2. PRINCIPAL'S LIABILITY FOR THE ACTS OF A CONTRACTOR

7.12 The nature of liability, when arising, is personal and not vicarious for the following reasons:

(a) The contractor (C) is engaged to produce a given result, the principal (P) having no power to direct the method of doing the work which is at C's discretion.

(b) Contractors, unlike servants, are more likely to be financially sound. They may even be more sound than their principals.

7.13 **Circumstance in which P is liable** may arise:

(a) when there is a breach of non-delegable duties, i.e. when there is a duty to see that proper care is taken.

(b) when there is a breach of the duty of reasonable care.

7.14 **NON-DELEGABLE DUTIES.** P may have a personal duty to see that proper care is taken.

(a) **P authorises or ratifies the tort.** The instigator of another's tort will always be liable whether the other is a servant, independent contractor, or agent. In *Ellis v. Sheffield Gas Co. (1853)*, P, without legal power, engaged C to dig a hole thereby creating and authorising a public nuisance. E fell over a heap of stones and the defendants were liable.

(b)   **P engages C to perform acts involving strict liability.** Examples include: the removal of support accorded to land or buildings *(Bower v. Peate (1876))*; extra-hazardous work such as in Rylands v. Fletcher or *Honeywill & Stein v. Larkin Bros. (1934)*, in which the plaintiffs secured permission to have photographs taken inside a theatre in which they had worked. The defendant photographers, using magnesium flares, set fire to the curtains. (At the time such photography was a serious fire risk.) Plaintiffs, though not themselves negligent and not an employer in the sense of being a master, were liable to the theatre owners as, having created the risk, they had a duty to see that proper care was taken. The plaintiffs sought an indemnity from the defendants.

(c)   **Creation of dangers on the highway.** This is public nuisance *(Penny v. Wimbledon UDC (1899))*.

(d)   **Statutes may oblige P to do the work in a particular way.** In *Hole v. Sittingbourne Railway (1861)*, contrary to statutory provision, C's defective work caused delays on a navigable river. P was liable as they should have seen that the work was properly done and in accordance with the obligations.

7.15   DUTY OF REASONABLE CARE. The P may carelessly appoint an incompetent contractor. Also P may, for want of care, not give proper instructions to C to enable the latter to avoid dangers.

7.16   Collateral negligence. P, unlike a master, does not become liable for the collateral negligence of their contractors *(Padbury v. Holliday & Greenwood Ltd. (1912))*. For P to be liable, the danger must be inherent in the work and not the mere performance of it.

3.   PRINCIPAL & AGENT

7.17   This relationship has little to do with vicarious liability. An agent may be a servant or a contractor. The main interest therefore centres on car owner/driver relationships outside master and servant situations.

7.18   Car owners are liable for the negligent driving of their agents but when, in non-servant cases, does agency arise?

(a)   **Owner present in the car.** In this situation, presence implies right of control. In *Samson v. Aitchison (1912)*, a prospective purchaser's son drove negligently but the passenger-owner had the right of control and was liable.

(b)   **Owner's purposes.** In *Ormrod v. Crosville (1953)* an owner asked his friend to drive his car from Birkenhead to Monte Carlo. The owner was to travel separately to join his friend for a holiday. The owner was liable for the friend's accident en route as the journey was for the owner's purpose.

But mere permission to drive does not create agency as the journey must be for the owner's purpose. The concern of the owner with the safe use of the vehicle is not enough to create a 'purpose'. In *Morgans v. Launchbury (1973)*, the defendant allowed her husband to go on a pub crawl but expected him to delegate the driving to someone else if unfit to drive. The husband's friend drove negligently killing the husband and injuring the plaintiff. The defendant was not vicariously liable as the journey was not for her 'purpose'. The House of Lords also rejected the notion that, in the case of a matrimonial car, almost any journey with either spouse as a passenger had a joint matrimonial purpose.

4. PARENTS' LIABILITY FOR CHILD

7.19   A child is responsible for his own torts and the parent will not be vicariously liable in the absence of agency or contract of service but the parent may be personally liable for lack of supervision. Examples:

(a)   *Bebee v. Sales (1916).* A young boy broke a window with an airgun which his father threatened to destroy. Later the plaintiff was injured by the boy's negligent use of the gun. The father was liable as, knowing of the danger, allowed the continued use of the gun.

(b)   *Donaldson v. McNiven (1961).* A thirteen year old was allowed to use a rifle provided he used it only in the cellar of the house. Unknown to the father, the boy used the gun in an alleyway and injured the plaintiff. The father, having taken reasonable steps to exercise control, was not liable.

CHAPTER 8

GENERAL DEFENCES AND LIMITATION

8.1   Reference has been made to defences to trespass and defamation in Chapter 4, and nuisance in Chapter 3. This chapter deals with other defences.

1. NECESSITY

8.2   A person may lawfully protect property and person even though an innocent person may suffer loss. In *Cope v. Sharpe (1912)* a gamekeeper, to protect his master's birds, set fire to heather on adjoining land to create a break in the face of fire. Held — no liability.

2. EXEMPTION CLAUSES

8.3   A defendant may sometimes plead that a contract term exempts him from, or reduces, his liability (see Chapter 11).

3. VOLENTI

8.4   **Volenti non fit injuria** (to him who is willing there can be no injury). A person, having knowledge of the nature and extent of the risk created by the defendant, cannot enforce a right which he has voluntarily waived or abandoned. Sometimes the maxim has been used to justify a different standard of care, particularly accidents at sporting events. At such events the standard of care is fixed in relation to what the average spectator is entitled to expect. Thus, there was no breach of duty in *Hall v. Brooklands Auto-Racing (1932)* when motor-racing was the spectacle. In *Wooldridge v. Summer (1962)* a photographer was injured by a rider's error of judgment which, in the circumstances, did not amount to negligence. More strictly, volenti applies to voluntary agreements to release defendants from the legal consequences of the unreasonable risks they have created.

8.5   **Important aspects of volenti:**

(a)   **Knowledge of a risk is not consent to it.** In *Smith v. Baker (1891)*, the plaintiff complained of a crane carrying rocks above him but he continued his employment. Later a falling rock injured him. His employers pleaded 'volenti' as he knew of the risk but continued working. The defence did not apply.

(b)   **The consent must be real.** It will not be genuine consent if the plaintiff has been deprived of freedom of choice by such as:

(i) **Economic pressure** — Often in employment cases, as in *Smith v. Baker (1891)*, this deprives the plaintiff of freedom of choice. Volenti hardly ever applies where the so-called 'voluntary act' is in the ordinary course of duty, unless the nature of the work necessitates danger. However, an employer is not obliged to either dismiss a worker or make the work safe when the employee runs a slight risk (e.g. dermatitis) because of the worker's particular susceptibility. The joint and flagrant disobedience of safety rules may be one instance where volenti defeats an employee. In *I.C.I. v. Shatwell (1965)*, the claim rested on vicarious liability for such a breach of a safety rule as the wrongdoing of a fellow worker was not bound to be obeyed.

(ii) **Legal duty** — This may apply to policemen and others in public service. In *Haynes v. Harwood (1935)*, a policeman rushed from his station to control horses attached to a van but carelessly unattended endangering a woman and children. The injured officer, being under a duty act, was not a volunteer.

(iii) **Moral and other constraints, including 'rescue'** — A moral constraint may be sufficient to remove freedom of choice. In *Morgan v. Aylen (1942)*, the plaintiff ran on to the road to save a child endangered by a negligent motor-cyclist. The plaintiff was not a volunteer.

Danger invites rescue so an injured rescuer cannot be said to have acted freely. A person, whose negligence creates danger, should appreciate that a third party may attempt a rescue. In *Baker v. Hopkins (1959)* a doctor died after descending a gas-filled well to rescue two workmen overcome by fumes. The volenti plea failed. As the negligence in such cases precedes the rescue, it is improbable that the plaintiff would have agreed to accept the risk of negligence. However, there are limitations on the rescue principle. Volenti may not succeed if there is no danger to others and the plaintiff's act is unreasonable. In *Cutler v. United Dairies (London) Ltd. (1933)*, C was injured when a horse and cart bolted into a field. C entered the field and was injured. His claim failed as, no one being in danger, his act was unreasonable. In *Sylvester v. Chapman (1935)*, S acted unreasonably when he went inside a barrier to extinguish a cigarette only to be mauled by a leopard.

8.6 **Volenti and the passengers of drunken drivers.** The question arises, as it did in *Dann v. Hamilton (1939)*, as to whether acceptance of a lift amounts to volenti. In that case it was held that it did not apply unless the drunkenness was so extreme as to equate to 'intermeddling with an unexploded bomb'. The Road Traffic Act 1972 S. 148(3) seeks to deprive the defendant of the volenti plea where the latter is sued in circumstances to which the compulsory insurance provisions apply. In *Ashton v. Turner (1982)*, 'volenti' was held to apply to a burglar who was a passenger in a get-away car driven by a drunken driver. The court may have been influenced by the **ex turpi causa** plea. Often the problem may be resolved by reference to contributory negligence *(Owens v. Brimmell (1977))*.

46

4. ACT OF GOD

8.7   This is of limited application and has been considered under *Rylands v. Fletcher (1868)* (see para. 5.6(c)).

5. STATUTORY AUTHORITY

8.8   This is mostly concerned with nuisance but is of general application.

6. CONTRIBUTORY NEGLIGENCE

8.9   At common law, a plaintiff who, even to a small extent, had contributed fault to his own injury, could be entirely defeated by the defence of contributory negligence. In *Butterfield v. Forrester (1809)*, the careless plaintiff ran into a pole carelessly placed in the road by the defendant. The plaintiff's contribution defeated his claim. *The last opportunity rule* mitigated the plaintiff's hardship by providing that, where both parties contributed negligence, he alone would be liable who had the last opportunity of avoiding the accident by reasonable care. In *Davies v. Mann (1842)*, the defendant carelessly drove into a donkey negligently tethered in the highway by the plaintiff. Held — defendant wholly liable. However, as an inflexible instrument the rule became obsolete. It could not be applied to highway collisions between fast-moving vehicles. Thus, in *Swadling v. Cooper (1931)* the House of Lords approved a direction — 'Whose negligence . . . substantially caused the injury?' to determine which of the parties was to be made liable. Even today if there is a sufficient separation of time, place or circumstances to enable a clear line to be drawn between the faults of the parties, only one may attract liability.

8.10   **Law Reform (Contributory Negligence) Act 1945.** This introduced apportionment of damages according to the degree of blame. Thus when both parties are at fault, the plaintiff's fault does not defeat his claim but damages are reduced according to his share of the responsibility. 'Fault' is defined as 'the negligence, breach of statutory duty or other act or omission which gives rise to liability in tort, or would apart from this Act, give rise to the defence of contributory negligence'. No reciprocal duty of care is necessary; the defendant must show:

(a)   the plaintiff failed to take reasonable care of his own safety in respect of the risk to which the defendant's negligence exposed him.

(b)   the plaintiff's failure contributed to his injury.

8.11   **Two contributions.** The plaintiff may contribute to the accident or his injury (or both).

(a)   **Contribution to the accident.** In *Baker v. Willoughby (1970)* the plaintiff failed to take evasive action when crossing in front of a negligently driven car that could clearly be seen. 50% of the blame attached to the plaintiff. In *Jones v. Livox Quarries Ltd. (1952)*, J, riding on the back of a traxcavator, was struck by a vehicle. J's damages were reduced as he had exposed himself to a foreseeable risk. His plea, that he had exposed himself only to the risk of being ejected and not crushed, failed. Had he been hit by a careless shot from a gun his negligence would have been inoperative.

The *principle of alternative danger* is relevant to 'contribution by the plaintiff':

(i)   The plaintiff may be excused for acting in the agony of the moment. In *Jones v. Boyce (1816)* the plaintiff, fearing that a fast-driven coach would overturn, jumped and broke his leg. He did not contribute to his injury and it was irrelevant that the coach did not actually overturn. The principle applies to emergencies generally even though created by third parties and may apply even when property is endangered.

(ii)   Defendants cannot necessarily expect the plaintiff to forfeit freedom of action in the face of risk. In *Clayards v. Dethick (1848)*, a cab driver's horse fell into an unfenced trench near the stable and died. The plaintiff was not negligent in attempting a task made difficult by the defendant's negligence. However, disproportionate risks are not excused under this 'dilemma' principle. In *Sayers v. Harlow UDC (1958)*, a faulty lock in a toilet caused S to try and climb out of a cubicle. She stood on a toilet roll holder and fell. Her carelessness in relying on the holder caused a 25% reduction in her damages.

(iii)   **Children.** A lower standard of care is expected. A child does not contribute through the carelessness of an accompanying adult.

(iv)   **Workmen.** The statutory duties of an employer are designed to protect even the inattentive so not every act of his will amount to contributory negligence.

(b)   **Contribution to the injury.** A plaintiff not in any way to blame for the accident may suffer a reduction in damages if, for want of care, he has contributed to the seriousness of the injury. Failure to wear crash helmets or use seat belts have affected motor-cycle and vehicle users respectively.

In *O'Connell v. Jackson (1972)* the plaintiff's damages were reduced as he did not wear a crash helmet. In *Froom v. Butcher (1976)*, the plaintiff's injuries would have been avoided had a seat belt been worn. His share of the blame was put at 25%. A smaller share would have been set if wearing a seat belt would have reduced the extent of the injuries as opposed to avoiding them. In *Owens v. Brimmell (1977)* no deduction was made on account of the plaintiff's failure to wear a seat belt. The outcome in terms of injury was unaffected by this failure which was therefore inoperative.

7.   LIMITATION OF ACTIONS

8.12   This is not really a defence but the right to sue lapses if the action is not brought within the period specified in the *Limitation Act 1980*.

8.13 **The general rule**, according to the Act, is that an action in tort must be brought within six years of the date the right accrues. The exception — when the damages claimed consist of, or include, an item for personal injuries, the period is three years.

8.14 **The accrual of the cause of action** is the moment the potential plaintiff is entitled to succeed against the potential defendant, e.g. in negligence, the cause of action accrues only when the damage is suffered. This may be simultaneous with the negligence (e.g. car accidents) or there may be an interval between the negligence or breach of statute and manifestation of the damage (e.g. the long-tail cases such as asbestosis). Time runs in all cases from time of damage, but special rules exist to overcome problems such as that in *Cartledge v. Jopling & Sons Ltd. (1963)*. A widow's claim failed after her husband's death from pneumoconiosis. The statutory period began to run when he first contracted the disease, at which time he remained ignorant of the disease (nor would it have been revealed by an X-ray). The period actually expired by the time the discovery was made.

8.15 **Claims involving personal injuries.** Time runs from time of damage or from the time of the plaintiff's knowledge of the damage. This remedies the injustice in Cartledge's case above. 'Date of knowledge' by S. 14(1) of the Act means the date on which the plaintiff first had knowledge of the following:

(a) that the injury was significant;

(b) that the injury was attributable wholly or partly to the alleged act or omission;

(c) the identity of the defendant;

(d) if it is alleged that the act or omission was that of a person other than the defendant, the identity of that person and the additional facts supporting the bringing of an action against the defendant (e.g. the plaintiff might wish to establish the existence of a master and servant relationship).

For (a) above, the injury is significant if the person would reasonably have considered it sufficiently serious to institute proceedings against a claimworthy defendant who accepted liability. 'Knowledge' includes knowledge which he should reasonably have been expected to acquire from facts (i) observable or ascertainable by him, (ii) ascertainable by him with the help of medical or other appropriate expert advice which it is reasonable for him to seek.

S. 33 of the Act gives the court discretion to **extend the time limits** if the three year period has expired. The court must regard all the circumstances of the case and such matters as the length of, and the reasons for, the delay, the effect of the delay on the cogency of the evidence etc. In *Cornish v. Kearly & Tonge Ltd. (1983)*, C was injured in July 1975 when a 250 lb. piece of beef fell on him. He felt pain from time to time but did not issue a writ until December 1981. His action was allowed as the reasons for the delay were reasonable; there was little reduction in the cogency of the evidence; C and his advisers acted promptly and reasonably; C was not unreasonable in not seeking legal advice until June 1981.

8.16   Latent damage in property and economic loss cases. In *Pirelli v. Oscar Faber & Partners (1983)*, the House of Lords held that the cause of action arose when the property damage occurred irrespective of whether it was discoverable by the plaintiff. The defendants negligently designed a chimney in which cracks must have appeared in 1970 but were not discovered until 1977 by which time the expiry of six years made the claim statute-barred. In the professional liability case of *Forster v. Oughtred & Co. (1982)*, the Court of Appeal held that time began to run from the time the plaintiff acted in reliance on the negligent advice and not when the financial loss was sustained.

The *Latent Damages Act 1986* tackles the problems of latent property damage by introducing a special extension allowing three years from the date on which the plaintiff discovered or ought reasonably to have discovered significant damage. The 'knowledge' aspects closely follow those referred to above in regard to personal injury claims. A further provision (S. 14(B)), a long-stop, bars all claims brought more than 15 years from the date of the defendant's negligence. The provisions override Pirelli and it would seem that in cases such as Forster's, the time will run from time of discoverability of financial loss. The 1986 Act came into force in September 1986 and does not apply to actions barred or commenced before that time.

8.17   Persons under a disability. If, when a cause of action accrues, the plaintiff is a minor, or is of unsound mind, the time (six or three years as the case may be) runs from the date the disability ends or death whichever occurs first. However, once time has begun to run, there will be no extension on account of supervening disability, subject, in personal injury cases to the court's discretion under S. 33 of the 1980 Act.

CHAPTER 9

LEGISLATION AND REMEDIES

1. REMEDIES

9.1 **DAMAGES** is the principal remedy for a tort, breach of contract or breach of duty and is it at the centre of the indemnity under liability policies. The principle is to compensate the plaintiff for the injury/damage. General damages may be recovered for pain and suffering, injury to health and personal inconvenience etc. and are of a kind presumed by law. Special damage must be expressly pleaded and proved and can be calculated with reasonable accuracy. The plaintiff is under a duty to mitigate his loss.

Personal injury cases

9.2 **Pain and suffering.** This entitles the plaintiff to compensation, for both actual and prospective suffering. If expectation of life has been reduced, the award may take account of the anguish caused by the plaintiff's awareness of this reduction. 'Loss of expectation of life' claims have been abolished (Administration of Justice Act 1982) and may only feature in this way. When death intervenes, a claim may account for the period up to the date of death. A permanently unconscious plaintiff has no claim for pain and suffering.

9.3 **Loss of amenities.** Compensation is recoverable for loss of faculty even for those plaintiffs who remain unaware of their loss. Damages may take account of subjective factors, e.g. deprivation of sporting pleasures, disfigurement, inability to walk etc.

9.4 **Loss of earnings**, both actual and prospective may be claimed. The latter is more difficult to quantify. Account is taken, inter alia, of the number of years work denied to the plaintiff, contingencies (e.g. unemployment), acceleration of payment, and a deduction is made for living expenses in the 'lost years' when life expectancy is reduced. Note that when the action is by a deceased's estate, no claim arises for loss of income for any period after the death (S. 4(2) Administration of Justice Act 1982). Certain deductions are made from any loss of earnings award; this includes half of the value of any rights in respect of sickness or invalidity benefit and the like for 5 years from the accrual of the cause of action (S. 2(1) Law Reform (Personal Injuries) Act 1948).

9.5 **Medical expenses** actually incurred may be the subject of special damages, while reasonable prospective expenses form part of the general damages.

9.6 **Other pecuniary losses,** e.g. cost of engaging domestic help, are recoverable. The list is open for any pecuniary loss arising.

Property damage cases

9.7 **Damage to property.** When property has been destroyed, the loss is the market value at the time of loss. Damages are also recoverable for loss of use pending replacement. When damage occurs the diminution in value is the measure and when goods are involved cost of repairs fixes the sum. Loss of use is again recoverable.

2. DEATH AS A CAUSE OF ACTION — FATAL ACCIDENTS ACT 1976

9.8 **No action in tort by a third party for another's death.** This common law rule has been partially eroded by exceptions now contained in the Fatal Accidents Act 1976 as amended. Certain relatives have a right of action. The common law continues to bar others, e.g. claims by employers following tortiously caused deaths of employees.

9.9 **The Act applies when:**

(a)   a right of action would have been available to the deceased had he lived *(Read v. G.E.R. (1868))*, but an action is admissible if the deceased had merely agreed to limit the amount of his claim *(Nunan v. Southern Railway (1924))*.

(b)   the party is within the class of protected relatives.

(c)   the relative concerned has suffered a pecuniary loss after the death.

9.10 **Relatives who can sue.** The range is fairly wide going from spouses to cousins. Unmarried 'cohabitors' together for two years may claim. A dependant relative may bring the action if there is no executor or administrator, or, there being one, he has failed to act, within 6 months of the death.

9.11 **Interests protected:**

(a)   **Bereavement** (by the Administration of Justice Act 1982). A claim for the benefit of a spouse (not former spouses or cohabitors) may include damages for bereavement. Parents suffering the loss of a minor, who has never been married, may also claim but in the case of an illegitimate minor only the mother may claim. The amount of claim varies from time to time by statutory instrument, the aim being to award one-half of average annual earnings.

(b)   **Loss of prospective pecuniary advantage.** The claim appears to be limited to the loss of the direct financial contribution to the dependant. Speculative prospect of gain is not enough. The gain may have been based on a legally enforceable right or have been entirely gratuitous. In all cases it must have accrued from a family (not business) relationship.

52

9.12 **Assessing damages** starts with wages less living expenses converted to a lump sum by a multiplier. Deductions are made for the immediate payment of a lump sum and for income tax. Dependants who incur funeral expenses may claim those expenses. The final sum is apportioned among them when there is more than one claim. If the deceased was partly to blame, contributory negligence applies. In assessing damages no account is taken of (i) re-marriage prospects of a widow; (ii) benefits accruing from the deceased's estate or otherwise (e.g. inheritance, insurance monies).

9.13 **Period of limitation.** Claims must be brought within three years of the death or 'knowledge' of the claiming relative, whichever is the later. Extensions may be granted under S. 33 Limitation Act 1980.

3. SURVIVAL OF ACTIONS —
LAW REFORM (MISCELLANEOUS PROVISIONS) ACT 1934

9.14 **At common law claims did not survive the death of an individual.** This rule prevented the deceased's personal representative from suing or being sued in regard to torts against or by the deceased prior to the intervention of death. Survival of causes of action is permitted under the above Act which provides — ' on the death of any person all causes of action subsisting against or vested in him, survive against, or, as the case may be, for the benefit of his estate'.

9.15 **The effect of the Act** enables the estate to claim damages for the period between the accrual of the cause of action and the death and may thus include pain and suffering, loss of amenity etc. Damages are calculated 'without reference to any loss or gain to the estate consequent upon the death' so annuities previously payable to the deceased and life insurance monies now payable will be disregarded. Awards under the 1934 Act are the same regardless of claims under the Fatal Accidents Act (under the latter there is to be no duplication of damages).

4. JOINT TORTS — CIVIL LIABILITY (CONTRIBUTION ACT) 1978

9.16 **Joint torts.** Damage may follow the torts of two or more defendants who may be (i) joint tortfeasors or, (ii) several concurrent tortfeasors.

9.17 **Joint tortfeasors** occurs where two (or more) parties are responsible for the same tort (e.g. master and servant). *Several concurrent tortfeasors* commit separate but coincidental torts resulting in the same or different damage to the same plaintiff. In *Drinkwater v. Kimber (1952)* a car passenger was injured due to the negligence of two drivers. (Also see *The Koursk* 1924.) In these cases the unit of damage was indivisible between the tortfeasors concerned.

9.18   The distinction is now less important — Both joint and several concurrent tortfeasors are liable for the whole damage, but following *Brinsmead v. Harrison (1872)*, a judgment against one tortfeasor barred a claim against another. No such bar existed in the case of concurrent tortfeasors as plaintiffs have always been at liberty to proceed against others after securing judgment against one. The rule in Brinsmead's case was abolished in 1935 when an Act also abolished the rule that there could be no contribution between tortfeasors. The current legislation is the Civil Liability (Contribution Act) 1978.

5.   THIRD PARTIES (RIGHTS AGAINST INSURERS) ACT 1930

9.19   The Third Party (Rights against Insurers) Act 1930 confers on third parties rights against insurers in the event of the insured becoming bankrupt or otherwise insolvent. Exhibit 5 sets out the position both before and after the Act. Before the Act where an insured tortfeasor with an obligation to pay damages was insolvent the insurance monies were added to the assets of the insolvent insured for distribution among creditors generally. This would increase the amount of dividend available to all creditors at the expense of the plaintiff whose share would inevitably fall short of the compensation due as he would rank equally with other creditors. In the simplified example of the Exhibit, the plaintiff receives 50p in the £ while the other creditors, who would have received nothing, now get 50p in the £.

9.20   How the Act works:

(a)   It gives the plaintiff the right to claim directly against the insurer when the insured is insolvent.

(b)   Policy conditions purporting to deny the plaintiff's claim are of no effect.

(c)   If the insurer's liability to the insured exceeds the third party liability, the insured's rights regarding the excess are unaffected by the Act.

(d)   Both the insured and the insurer must give insurance details to any party seeking the benefit of the Act.

(e)   No action lies under the Act if the insured defendant has been dissolved *(Bradley v. Eagle Star (1988))*.

9.21   Rights of the third party are no greater than those of the insured. Defences (e.g. breach of utmost good faith) available against the insured hold good against the third party to defeat or limit his claim. In *Farrell v. National Motor (1934)*, a bankrupt was guilty of non-disclosure. As he could not have been indemnified, the third party had no claim under the Act.

9.22   Rights and not liabilities are transferred. In *Murray v. Legal & General (1969)*, M claimed £1,750 plus £186 costs. The insurers were not entitled to set off premium arrears of £1,708 against the claim as it is rights and not liabilities that are transferred to the third party.

6. ADMINISTRATION OF JUSTICE ACT 1969

9.23   S. 22 made it compulsory to add interest to damages in personal injury cases.

EXHIBIT 5

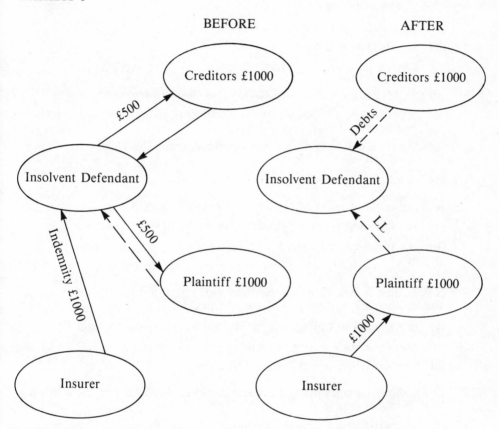

THIRD PARTIES (RIGHTS AGAINST INSURERS) ACT 1930

- Third party acquires rights against insurer when insured is insolvent.
- Third party's rights no greater than those of insured.
- Policy conditions to the contrary of no effect.
- Rights of insured regarding excess not affected.
- Rights and not liabilities transferred.
- No rights if insured dissolved.

MULTIPLE CHOICE QUESTIONS

Choose the alternative which provides the best solution or completes the sentence most satisfactorily.

1. "Loss of expectation of life" claims:
   (a) have been abolished by statute;
   (b) are fixed at £3,500;
   (c) are not permitted as a part of "pain and suffering".

2. An insolvent insured breached the duty of utmost good faith:
   (a) a third party's claim under the Third Party (Rights Against Insurers) Act is not affected;
   (b) the breach defeats a third party claiming under the Third Party (Rights Against Insurers) Act;
   (c) Neither of the above.

3. A dependant has no claim under the Fatal Accidents Act if:
   (a) the deceased had no right of claim at the time of death;
   (b) the deceased had agreed to a limitation on his right of claim;
   (c) claim is not brought within 6 months of the death.

4. A passenger is injured by the negligence of his own driver (80% to blame) and another driver (20%) to blame, the passenger:
   (a) must claim in full against the driver "substantially to blame";
   (b) must sue both drivers;
   (c) can sue either driver for the full amount.

5. In assessing damages under the Fatal Accident Act which of the following must be disregarded?
   (a) re-marriage prospects of a widow;
   (b) funeral expenses;
   (c) deceased's wages.

CHAPTER 10

PREMISES, HOTELS, BAILMENTS

PREMISES

In this area distinctions are made between (a) occupiers and non-occupiers; and (b) liability to those on the premises and those adjacent to the premises.

1. OCCUPIERS' LIABILITY

10.1 Common law liability of occupiers to visitors depended on the status of the visitor.

(a) **Licensees**, those with mere permission to enter, needed only to be warned of concealed dangers.

(b) **Invitees**, persons entering in pursuit of a common interest with the occupier (e.g. customer entering the occupier's shop) were owed a duty of reasonable care.

(c) **Trespassers** were owed no duty except that an occupier had a duty not to inflict injury intentionally or recklessly.

10.2 **The Occupiers' Liability Act 1957** combined licensees and invitees into the single category of 'lawful visitors' owed by the occupier the **common duty of care**. The duty arises from dangers from the land and not the activities carried out therein. Liability goes beyond personal injury and includes damage to the property of visitors.

(a) **The common duty of care** is the 'duty to take such care as in all the circumstances of the case is reasonable to see that the visitor will be reasonably safe in using the premises for the purpose for which . . . invited or permitted . . . to be there'. Points of guidance are set out below:

(i) **Children** — S. 2(3)(a) an occupier must be prepared for children to be less careful than adults. Derelict machinery, for example, may endanger a child but not an adult. Also the occupier should appreciate the effect of items of 'allurement'.

(ii) **Tradesmen** — S. 2(3)(b) . . . visitors exercising their trade (e.g. electricians) ought to appreciate and guard against risks incidental to their trade. In *Roles v. Nathan (1963)*, the occupier was not liable when two chimney sweeps died following carbon monoxide poisoning while sealing a hole in a chimney when the boiler was alight.

(iii) **Warnings** — S. 2(4)(a) . . . a warning will absolve an occupier if it is enough to make the visitor reasonably safe. To warn a veterinary surgeon, who needs to attend to a sick animal at the end of the yard, that he may fall into a tank is unlikely to be sufficient to make him reasonably safe.

(iv) **Assumption of the risk** — S. 2(1) . . . the duty may be extended, restricted or modified by agreement or otherwise unless, as in the Unfair Contract Terms Act 1977, the occupier's ability to do so is restricted. This Act applies primarily to 'business liability' and provides that liability for death or personal injury caused by negligence cannot be excluded or restricted. S. 2(5) preserves the defence of volenti and the private occupier may use it. Also S. 2(3) shows that the Law Reform (Contributory Negligence) Act 1945 applies.

(v) **Liability for the acts of independent contractors** — S. 2(4) . . . the occupier is not liable for damage arising from the faulty work of contractors but liability may arise if the occupier unreasonably entrusted the work to a contractor. Also the occupier will be liable if he fails to take reasonable steps to see that the work is properly done.

(vi) **Liability in contract** — S. 5(1) . . . where a person enters under contract and the contract is silent on the matter, the common duty of care will be implied. If the contract provides for greater protection the higher standard applies.

(vii) **Persons entering under a duty or power** — S. 2(6) . . . those entering under right conferred by law are to be treated as permitted by the occupier to be there.

10.3 Occupiers' Liability to non-visitors. The Occupiers' Liability Act 1984 governs liability to trespassers; persons entering under access agreement or order; persons using a private right of way. The duty owed is still usefully illustrated by *British Railways Board v. Herrington (1972)* in which the House of Lords established the 'common duty of humanity' owed by occupiers to trespassers. The duty arose if the occupier knew of the trespasser's presence or likelihood thereof. The duty to act 'humanely' was more subjective than normal in that the financial resources of the defendant were considered. The law appeared more tolerant of impoverished defendants than wealthy ones. Other factors to be considered included: age of trespasser, kind of land, time of the accident, ease of access for trespass and the extent of the danger. In *Herrington's* case B.R.B's neglected fence separated a rail line from a playfield. A six-year old went through the fence on to the line and was injured. There was a strong probability of such trespass and the failure to consider safety was culpable, especially given B.R's financial resources.

The statutory duty of the Act is broadly similar to the common law duty laid down in Herrington. The new duty (S. 1(4)) is to take such care as is reasonable in all the circumstances to see that the non-visitor is not injured on the premises by the danger concerned. What constitutes reasonable care varies according to circumstances and takes into account the nature and character of the entry, age of entrant, extent of risk and cost of precautions. S. 1(3) deals with the existence of the duty to non-visitors by providing that it is owed if the occupier:

(a)   Knows of the danger and has reasonable ground to believe it exists.

(b)   Knows or reasonably believes that the non-visitor is in the vicinity of the danger (whether he has lawful authority or not).

(c)   The risk is one against which, in the circumstances, he may reasonably be expected to offer some protection.

The duty is discharged if reasonable steps are taken to warn of, or discourage persons from incurring the risk. No duty is owed to those willingly accepting the risk.

S. 2 of the 1984 Act modifies the Unfair Contract Terms Act 1977 S. 1(3). It redefines 'business liability' by excluding persons obtaining access to premises for recreation or education.

2. NON-OCCUPIERS

The approach adopted is to identify the parties and describe their liabilities while identifying the source thereof.

10.4   **Repairing landlords.** Landlords are not generally liable for the safety of their premises (but see private nuisance). However, those with obligations or rights relating to repair are liable for defects provided they know or ought to know of the defect in question (Defective Premises Act S. 4). The repair obligations or rights may arise by:

(a)   by a term in the lease.

(b)   by statute, S. 8 and Ss. 11/12 Landlord & Tenant Act 1985. The former provides that with, 'low rented' premises, the house will be kept fit for human habitation. Ss. 11/12 oblige the landlord to carry out structural repairs and provide installations for sanitation, the supply of water, gas, and electricity for houses let for tenancies not exceeding 7 years.

(c)   a right, regardless of obligation, to enter and effect repairs but such right does not impose an obligation to the tenant, where the latter is obliged by lease to do repairs, for injuries due to defect in the premises.

What duty and to whom? The duty is to all persons reasonably expected to be affected by defects within the repair obligation for resultant personal injury or damage to property. The duty is wide, extending to trespassers and those outside the premises.

10.5   **Vendor/non-builder.** If an owner has done no work in relation to his premises he is not liable under common law or the Defective Premises Act for harm caused after disposal of the premises by sale or lease — 'caveat emptor' applies. This is so even if the owner knows of the defect (provided it is not created by him) which he does not repair or warn of.

10.6   Vendor/builder of new houses. The builder was not liable for predisposal negligence once he had disposed of the premises by sale or lease. S. 1, Defective Premises Act 1972 now imposes a duty on builders to build dwellings in a workmanlike and professional manner with proper materials so that the dwelling, when completed, will be fit for human habitation. The duty is owed by others in the building process (e.g. architects, local authorities). S. 3, Defective Premises Act 1972 provides that sale or disposal does not abate the duty, thus removing 'caveat emptor' in this context. The duty is owed to persons ordering the work and those who subsequently acquire an interest in the dwelling. S. 1, however, does not apply to dwellings when the purchaser is protected by an approved scheme (e.g. National House Building Council Scheme). The Act dictates that the three/six year limitation periods run from time of completion (not date of damage or knowledge thereof).

10.7   Non-vendor/builder. Where a builder is not a vendor (or lessor) of a house, he may be liable on grounds of negligence following principles established in Donoghue v. Stevenson relating to manufacturers of defective products.

In *Sharpe v. Sweeting & Sons Ltd. (1963)*, a builder of a council house was liable to the tenant's wife although the accident was 8 years after he built it. Liability is based on common law principles and is not confined to houses and is subject to the normal limitation periods.

10.8   Professional advisers may be liable in contract, in negligence, or, as noted, under S. 1 of the Defective Premises Act.

10.9   Local authorities may be liable under S. 1 of the Act but *Dutton v. Bognor Regis (1972)* had earlier shown that liability could arise at common law. A building inspector negligently certified that a new house complied with a byelaw on foundations. The authority was liable to a subsequent purchaser for subsidence damage occurring two years later.

3.   HOTELS

10.10   Two types of establishment. As special liabilities attach to one type but not the other, it is necessary to distinguish between **inns** and all other hotels, referred to for convenience as **'private hotels'**.

10.11   What is an inn? Defined in the Hotel Proprietors Act 1956 . . . 'an establishment held out by the proprietor as offering food, drink, and, if so required, sleeping accommodation, without special contract, to any traveller presenting himself . . . who appears able and willing to pay . . . and who is in a fit state to be received'. It is how the proprietor runs the establishment that determines its status. If he accepts **'all and sundry'**, subject only to willingness to pay, and, fitness to be received, and provides the facilities stated, then he is an innkeeper. In consequence he must:

(i)   not refuse reasonable refreshment at any hour of the day or night;

(ii)   not refuse accommodation if it is available in the public bedrooms;

(iii)   accept special responsibility for guests' effects.

10.12 Innkeeper's common law liability for guest's effects. He was strictly liable at comon law for the effects of all travellers, regardless of the services they sought. The liability was unlimited and intended to deter innkeepers from stealing directly or by way of collusion. The strict liability covered all property of the traveller within the shelter of the inn. Certain common law defences were, as now, available.

10.13 The Effect of the Hotel Proprietors Act 1956. It does not change the nature of the liability — it remains strict — but limits of liability are introduced and the 'strict liability' becomes confined to 'guests' effects'. The Act also removes strict liability in regard to certain forms of property.

Guests' effects. A guest is any person who has booked sleeping accommodation. Liability for loss or damage to the effects of such a person is strict. There is no longer strict liability for the effects of others, e.g. travellers calling for refreshment only. Liability in connection with their property may arise on grounds of negligence or out of a contract of bailment according to normal principles.

(a) **Financial limits** — Liability is limited to £50 any one article and £100 any one guest, but the innkeeper loses entitlement to such limits if he fails to display the notice set out in the Schedule of the Act in a conspicuous place. Moreover, these limits do not apply:

　　(i)　where the property is stolen, lost or damaged through default or neglect of the proprietor or his staff.

　　(ii)　where the property was deposited for safekeeping with the proprietor or authorised servant, and, if so required, in a sealed or fastened container.

　　(iii)　where the property was offered for safekeeping but refused by the proprietor or his servant.

(b) **No strict liability for certain forms of property** — There is no strict liability as an innkeeper for loss or damage to any vehicle or contents thereof, or any horse or other live animal or its harness or equipment. The innkeeper may still be liable on grounds of negligence or bailment.

(c) **The duration of strict liability** — This begins to run from midnight before the guest arrives and ends midnight after his departure. e.g. for goods left for collection a week after departure the ordinary rules of negligence and bailment (if applicable) will apply from midnight after departure. This is reasonable as it becomes more of a storage than travel risk.

10.14 Defences — The innkeeper, who brings the loss within the following, avoids all liability:

(i)　Act of God.

(ii)　Action of Queen's enemies but the innkeeper remains liable for riot damage.

(iii)　Negligence or misconduct of the guest. It would be unreasonable to make the innkeeper liable for loss caused by the guest.

10.15 Three possible situations for the innkeeper. Any loss can be brought under one of three headings, full liability; no liability; limited liability. See Exhibit 6.

EXHIBIT 6

HOTEL PROPRIETORS

HOTELS

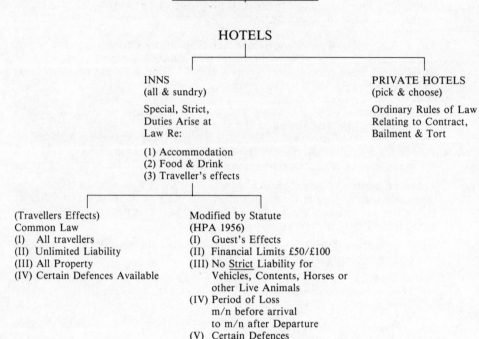

INNS
(all & sundry)

Special, Strict,
Duties Arise at
Law Re:

(1) Accommodation
(2) Food & Drink
(3) Traveller's effects

PRIVATE HOTELS
(pick & choose)

Ordinary Rules of Law
Relating to Contract,
Bailment & Tort

(Travellers Effects)
Common Law
(I)   All travellers
(II) Unlimited Liability
(III) All Property
(IV) Certain Defences Available

Modified by Statute
(HPA 1956)
(I)   Guest's Effects
(II) Financial Limits £50/£100
(III) No <u>Strict</u> Liability for
      Vehicles, Contents, Horses or
      other Live Animals
(IV) Period of Loss
      m/n before arrival
      to m/n after Departure
(V)   Certain Defences

THREE SITUATIONS

IDENTIFIED

(A) <u>Full Liability</u>

(i)   Innkeeper etc.
      Fault/Neglect
(ii) Property Deposited
      for Safekeeping
(iiii) Offered for Safe-
      keeping, but
      refused
(iv) Notice in
      Pursuance of Act
      not Displayed

(B) <u>No Liability</u>

(i)   Plaintiff at Fault
(ii) Act of God
(iii) Action of Queen's
      Enemies

(C) <u>Limited Liability</u>

All cases not coming
under A or B
(i)   £50 one Article
(ii) £100 one Guest
      provided the
      Notice is dis-
      played at or near
      Reception Desk

NB Cars etc.
Liability not strict
determined by ordi-
nary legal principles

62

10.16 Private hotels (establishments other than inns) — liability is governed by the ordinary rules relating to contract, bailment and tort. Principal features:

(i)   they can 'pick and choose' their customers (compare with inns — open to 'all and sundry'). Those establishments that indicate 'no children', 'no football parties' are picking and choosing and cannot therefore be inns. Private hotels cannot base their refusal on grounds of race, religion or ethnic origin (Race Relations Act).

(ii)   services may be more limited (e.g. restaurants not providing sleeping accommodation cannot be inns).

(iii)   Bailment will arise whenever goods are deposited for safekeeping and could even arise when a waiter takes a customer's coat to hang up. Liability under bailment following normal rules is considered in the next section.

4. BAILMENTS

10.17 Bailment arises when one person entrusts goods to another on the understanding that they will later be returned or otherwise accounted for (e.g. car in garage for servicing, but liability for jewellery deposited for safekeeping with an innkeeper is not founded on bailment).

10.18 Different types of bailee

(a)   **Bailees for reward** are paid for their services (e.g. dry cleaners). **Gratuitous bailees**, e.g. taking care of a friend's property when he is on holiday, receive no payment. A higher standard of care is expected of a bailee for reward, whose responsibility arises out of contract but gratuitous bailees, receiving no consideration, can only be liable in tort. In bailment for reward the standard varies according to the circumstances, more being expected of a jeweller than a shoe repairer.

      Bailees for reward may use contracts to:

(i)   extend their liability (even to the point where they become 'insurers').

(ii)   exclude or restrict their liability (subject to the Unfair Contract Terms Act 1977).

      Otherwise he is responsible for loss or damage unless he can show he was not at fault. He discharges this onus of proof if he can show that he took all reasonable precautions.

      Liability for the acts of servants arises for the acts (including dishonest ones) of servants 'performing classes of acts they are employed to do'. In *Morris v. Martin & Sons (1966)* a fur coat was stolen by the servant entrusted with the cleaning — employers liable.

(b)   **Gratuitous bailees** must show they adopted the standard of care a reasonable man would have for the safety of his own property.

10.19 The overriding consideration in bailment cases. Whether in all the circumstances of the case sufficient care was taken.

5.   CARRIAGE

10.20 This type of bailment is often covered by standard form contracts. Carriers by land may be (a) common carriers, or, (b) private carriers.

(a)   **Common carriers** carry goods for 'all and sundry' paying a reasonable charge. He may be a common carrier of a particular product over a particular route, but by limiting the service to a particular sector of the community he becomes a private carrier.

(b)   **A common carrier's liability at common law for the goods is strict,** the only defences being action of Queen's enemies, Act of God, fault of the owner of the goods, or inherent vice. Restrictions on this liability are provided by the Carriers Act 1830. Railways are not common carriers and road hauliers normally carry under the Road Haulage Associations Conditions of Carriage (or other standard contract).

10.21 **The liability of private carriers** may depend on a standard form of contract, but otherwise as a bailee, a private carrier is liable on grounds of negligence unless he can rebut the presumption.

CHAPTER 11

MANUFACTURERS' & SUPPLIERS' LIABILITY

11.1 Product liability

Both suppliers and manufacturers are exposed to the risk of injury or damage, for which liability may attach, arising from products supplied or manufactured. This liability may arise in contract, tort, or under statute.

1. CONTRACTUAL LIABILITY

11.2 Contractual liability. The common law rule in contracts for the sale of goods is 'caveat emptor' — let the buyer beware. Nothing obliges the seller to point out the disadvantages of his product. This is so even if silence is misleading but the seller must not induce the contract by misrepresentation.

11.3 The Sale of Goods Act 1979 modifies this situation by introducing certain implied conditions (Ss. 12-15). In the present context the implied conditions as to 'merchantable quality' (S. 14(2)) and 'fitness for purpose' (S. 14(3)) are the most important. Remedies for breach of these conditions are available only for actual buyers enjoying privity of contract with the supplier/seller. If a third party *(Donoghue v. Stevenson (1932))* is injured by a defective product there will be no remedy by way of contract.

(a) **'Merchantable quality'.** When a seller sells in the course of business it is implied that the goods are of merchantable quality but there is no such condition (i) regarding defects drawn to the buyer's attention when the contract is made; (ii) if the buyer examines the goods, regarding defects that the examination ought to reveal. In private sales (e.g. one insurance clerk sells another his car) there is no such implied condition. Merchantable quality means 'fit for the purpose for which products of that kind are commonly bought as it is reasonable to expect, having regard to the description applied to them, the price (if relevant) and all other relevant circumstances' (e.g. a new car at full price with a scratched wing would not be of merchantable quality).

(b) **'Fitness for purpose'.** Where a seller sells in the course of business and the buyer expressly or by implication makes known to the seller any particular purpose for which the goods are being bought, it is implied that the goods are reasonably fit for the purpose intended whether or not that is the purpose for which the goods are commonly supplied. There is no implied condition where the buyer does not rely, or it is unreasonable to rely, on the seller's skill or judgment. As noted, only 'business sellers' are affected and 'goods supplied' includes containers.

Liability for breach of the above conditions is strict. The seller may not have been at fault but he will be strictly liable to the actual buyer for any breach i.e. by refunding money or replacing 'shoddy products' and paying damages for the injurious nature of the products.

(c) **Analogous contracts.** Identical terms (see (a) and (b) above) are implied in hire purchase contracts (Consumer Credit Act 1974) and similar conditions in contracts where ownership in goods is transferred (e.g. exchange, work and materials) and into contracts where possession in goods passes (e.g. hire) (Supply of Goods and Services Act 1982). The 1982 Act also deals with services in areas relating to reasonableness as to price, time, and care.

(d) **Exemption clauses and the implied conditions.** Until 1973 a seller could contract out of 'merchantability' and 'fitness for purpose'. Electrical appliance suppliers often gave guarantees (replace parts over a twelve month period) but contracted out of the more valuable Sale of Goods Act rights. Ss. 6 and 7 UCTA, as noted, renders void any attempt to exclude the implied conditions (merchantability and fitness for purpose) in consumer sales. In non-consumer sales such exemptions will be unenforceable unless shown by the seller to be fair and reasonable. If a chartered accountant buys a micro-computer for professional use that is a non-consumer sale. If he purchases one for use at home by the family that is a consumer sale.

(e) **The chain of supply.** Although the retailer with a strict liability when making a consumer sale cannot exempt himself, he has rights of recovery against his own supplier. Dealings between retailers and their suppliers are non-consumer sales and therefore the retailer (or anyone in the chain of supply with a business supplier) may find the right of recovery blocked by way of an exemption clause provided it survives the test of reasonableness.

2.   LIABILITY OF MANUFACTURERS

11.4   Liability of manufacturers. A manufacturer's liability may arise through:

(a) **Contract of sale.** Liability is to the immediate purchaser only. The position in regard to implied terms and exemption clauses is as noted in the previous section.

(b) **Collateral contracts or guarantees** — Manufacturers' guarantees are capable of drawing the manufacturer into collateral contracts with the consumer while the latter makes a contract of sale with a retailer. The promise of guarantees may constitute the consideration given to the consumer in return for the latter entering into a contract of sale with an intermediate supplier of the product. Liability under the collateral contract is to the purchaser/consumer only. The guarantees cannot in the case of consumer goods contain exclusions of the manufacturers' liability in negligence (S. 5, UCTA) nor can they indicate that a buyer cannot rely on rights under the Sale of Goods Act 1979.

(c)   *The Consumer Protection Act 1961* **and** *The Consumer Safety Act 1978* introduced criminal sanctions aimed at preventing defective goods coming on to the market. A breach of duty is actionable as is a breach of any obligation imposed by a prohibition order or notice. The 1978 Act enables the government to regulate to set specific standards for specific goods (those considered hazardous). Part II of the Consumer Protection Act 1987 introduces a general safety requirement obliging suppliers of consumer products to supply products that are reasonably safe. Any relevant standards will be among the circumstances to be considered in deciding whether the goods are reasonably safe. Criminal sanctions are imposed for any breach.

        S. 6 Health & Safety at Work etc. Act is noted as it imposes duties on designers, manufacturers, importers, suppliers, erectors and installers. Although it does not apply to articles supplied for consumer use, many articles intended for consumer use will be used at work. The Consumer Protection Act 1987 requires the exercise of reasonable foresight in product design and construction so amending the duty under S. 6 HSWA.

(d)   **Negligence.** *Donoghue v. Stevenson (1932)* applied 'the neighbour principle' to the manufacturer/third party-consumer relationship. The injured party had not purchased the ginger beer (it had been purchased for her), thus she is distinguished from the purchaser by the term 'third party consumer'. Consequently a manufacturer who sells a product in such a form that he intends it to reach the ultimate consumer in the same form, with no possibility of intermediate examination, and knowing that a lack of care in preparing or putting up the product will result in injury or damage to the consumer, owes a duty to the consumer to take reasonable care. In practical terms, negligence may arise:

(i)   in design;

(ii)   in the quality control system;

(iii)   in marketing, e.g. misleading instructions;

(iv)   from failure to recall a dangerous product.

        The duty is owed to anyone within the neighbour principle and not just consumers third party or otherwise, e.g. storemen handling the goods are entitled to protection.

        Definition of a manufacturer is broad and the duty is also owed by designers, assemblers and repairers, i.e. anyone capable of creating the defect or negligently overlooking it.

        Intermediate examination of the product is unlikely to occur with such as bottles of ginger beer as they pass down the chain of supply. Where such an examination is expected and likely to reveal the defect, a subsequent distributor and not the manufacturer may be liable. In *Kubach v. Hollands (1937)* a chemical carried a warning that it should be tested before use. The distributor failed to do the test or warn the school to which it was supplied. The distributor was liable for injury to a schoolgirl. Mere opportunity to inspect does not exonerate the manufacturer. In *Herschtaal v. Stewart & Arden (1939)* H was injured when, the day after hiring the defendant's car, a wheel came off. An inspection was not expected or contemplated. In *Farr* *v. Butters (1932),* B sold defective crane parts to a firm whose experienced employee observed the defect but risked using the crane only to be killed in an ensuing accident. The manufacturers expected that a pre-use examination would be carried out and so were not liable. Suppliers/distributors will not be liable unless they could reasonably have been expected to examine the product and discover its defect.

(e)   *The Consumer Protection Act 1987,* Part I of which gives effect to the EEC Directive on Product Liability. It is **in addition** to any existing contractual or tortious or other liability and it is probable that the majority of product defect cases will still be dealt with by the law described above. No liability is imposed under the Act in respect of products first supplied before 1 March 1988.

(i)   S. 2 sets out the important **general principle**. Where any damage is caused by a defect in a product every producer (see (vi) below) shall be liable unless a defence applies. On five key points (damage, causation, defect, product, producer) the onus of proof attaches to the plaintiff but it is for the defendant to show that a defence applies. Liability is strict in that the need to prove negligence is removed. This already applies to the actual buyer under sale of goods law. The Act provides the same rights to anyone injured by a defective product, whether or not the product was sold to them.

(ii)   S. 3 defines **defective product** as one where the safety of the product is not such as persons generally are entitled to expect. The test is objective and, given that safety is a relative concept, some form of cost/benefit analysis arises to enquire if the benefit of the product outweighs the cost of making it safer. The Act mentions presentation, the reasonably expected use, and the time the product was put into circulation. Age of the item becomes relevant as the safety standard applicable will be that at the date of supply and not at the date of damage or of earlier manufacture.

(iii)   S. 4 sets out six **defences**. There will be no liability if:
● the defendant did not supply the product (e.g. if it was stolen or a counterfeit copy).
● the state of scientific and technical knowledge at time of supply was not such that a producer of products of the same description might be expected to have discovered the defect if it had existed in his products while they were under his control (the 'development risks' defence). A number of EEC countries have not included the defence in their legislation.
● the defect was caused by complying with the law.
● the defect was not in the product at the time it was supplied (e.g. proper instructions or warnings may be detached by the final supplier).
● the supplier is not in business (e.g. sales by private individuals of second-hand goods are excluded but a business selling used equipment is not covered by the defence).

● the defect is due to end-product design. Thus a component manufacturer, if the defect is due to the design of the subsequent product or to compliance with the instructions from the producer of that produce, escapes liability.

The extent of liability could be affected by any contributory negligence on the part of the plaintiff.

(iv) S. 5 sets out the **damage** covered. It includes death or personal injury. Also covered is loss of, or damage to **private property** (including land) provided the loss exceeds £275. Damage to the product is excluded as is the product in which the defective product is a component. Other types of loss (e.g. damage to commercial property and pure economic loss) must be pursued against the manufacturer on the basis of negligence. The plaintiff must show **causation** S. 2(1), i.e. on balance of probabilities, the defect caused the damage.

(v) S. 1(2) defines **product** as any goods, including a product comprised in another product, either as a component or raw material. It includes electricity. The Act does not apply to game or agricultural produce which has not undergone any industrial process but processed products are not excluded as the processing itself could cause a defect. Buildings are not covered although individual goods from which they are built (e.g. bricks and beams) are covered. Thus, unprocessed agricultural products apart, all other goods, including those used at places of work, are included.

(vi) Ss. 2 & 1(2) show that the term **producer** can apply to all suppliers in the chain. The following may be liable:
● **Producers**, i.e. manufacturers of the product, components, or suppliers of raw materials.
● **Importers**, i.e. anyone importing into the EEC to supply it to another in the course of business.
● **'Own branders'**: suppliers who put their own name on the product and give the impression that they are producers.
● **'Forgetful suppliers'.** If any supplier of a product is unable to meet a victim's request to identify one or more persons in the three foregoing categories or identify his own supplier, then he will be liable.

There is joint and several liability between all these potential defendants.

(vii) **The Limitation Period** requires that proceedings must begin within three years of the date on which the plaintiff or injured person becomes aware of the cause of action but an injured person cannot sue under Part I of the Act ten years after the defective product was supplied by the producer.

(viii) **S. 7. Exclusion and limitation clauses** are void and override the provisions of UCTA including S. 2(2) which provides a test of reasonableness.

(ix) **Ceiling on liability.** The UK has not taken the option to set a financial limit on the producer's liability for damage.

3. EXCLUSION OF LIABILITY

11.5   Liability of manufacturers and suppliers is generally capable of being extended or restricted by contract. Emphasis here is upon the use of exemption clauses upon which a defendant may sometimes rely by way of defence.

11.6   **Exemption clauses** exempt or restrict the liability of one of the parties, usually the party who draws up the contract (e.g. a dry cleaner may seek to exempt himself from liability for loss or damage to a customer's goods). An **indemnity clause** is one under which one party (e.g. a sub-contractor) agrees to make good the losses of another (e.g. his principal).

11.7   **Obstacles against the use of exemption clauses.** Obstacles have frequently been placed in the way of those seeking to exempt, restrict or pass on, their liability. The courts have often been prompted by the fact that parties to a contract may not have been on equal bargaining terms resulting in unfairness to the weaker party. These 'obstacles' are summarised below:

(a)   **Clause held not to be a part of the contract.** A contract is formed when the acceptance is communicated to the offeror. Thereafter neither party can introduce new terms in the absence of fresh consideration. In *Olley v. Marlborough Court Ltd. (1949)* the contract was made at the reception desk so the notice, in the bedroom purporting to restrict the hotel's liability for loss of valuables, was not a part of the contract and did not bind O. In another case passengers on a flight were seated when a notice excluding liability was handed to them! The opportunity of acceptance or rejection is vital.

(b)   **The contra proferentum rule.** Ambiguity in a clause will be construed strictly against the party who drafted the clause. General terms e.g. 'no liability accepted', are not construed as excluding liability for specific torts. In *Smith v. S. Wales Switchgear (1978)* an indemnity clause failed to avail the respondents as there was no express provision against their own negligence. The term 'whatsoever' was not treated by the House of Lords as an equivalent reference to negligence.

(c)   **Acceptance of term induced by misrepresentation.** In *Curtis v. Chemical Cleaning (1951)*, a cleaning firm's document read 'the company is not liable for any damage howsoever arising'. A customer about to deposit a wedding dress was told, on enquiry, that the phrase meant that the company did not accept liability for damage to the sequins. When returned to the customer the dress was stained and the company, having misrepresented the effects of the clause, was liable.

(d)   **The privity rule.** A person not a party to the contract cannot benefit from an exemption clause within it. In *Scruttons Ltd. v. Midland Silicones Ltd. (1961)*, stevedores were not protected by a contract between the shippers and the shipowners under which liability was limited.

(e)   **A 'fundamental breach' may prevent reliance on an exemption clause.** A party who steps outside the four corners of his contract may be prevented from relying upon restrictions within it. In *Harbutt's Plasticine v. Wayne Tank & Pump Co. Ltd. (1970)*, WT contracted to design and supply a flow system for the factory. They sought to limit their liability to £2,330, the value of the contract. They breached their contract by supplying a defective system, which, unfortunately, was through the negligence of a workman switched on. A fire resulted and damage amounted to £151,420. The breach of contract denied WT the protection of the clause under which they sought to limit their liability. However, there is no doctrine of fundamental breach. It is a matter of construction whether an exemption clause is wide enough to cover a fundamental breach, but there seems to be a presumption that an exemption clause only avails a party who is substantially carrying out his obligations. In *Photoproductions Ltd. v. Securicor (1980)* a patrolman caused a fire at premises he was employed to protect, thus putting his employers in breach of contract. Despite the breach they were able to rely on an exemption clause which was construed as being wide enough to cover the breach. The parties remain free to draw up contracts accordingly but will, in certain circumstances, be constrained by the Unfair Contract Terms Act 1977.

(f)   **The Unfair Contract Terms Act 1977** (UCTA for short) regulates business liability (activities in the course of business or occupation of business premises). It also covers breach of implied obligations in sale of goods and hire purchase contracts. Insurance contracts are exempt from the Act, the key points of which are:

(i)   **Exclusion of liability for negligence leading to death or injury** is not permitted by a business by way of contract or notice (S. 2(1)). In other cases businesses are permitted to exclude liability for other forms of loss (e.g. property damage) so caused if it is fair and reasonable to do so (S. 2(2)).

(ii) **Exclusion of liability for breach of contract.** S. 3 protects consumers as well as 'small businesses'. This small business protection operates whenever a business enters into a contract on the standard contract form of the other party. The underlying assumption is that there is unequal bargaining power and that, generally, the firms, with little or no opportunity to negotiate, are confronted with 'take or leave it' situations. Such firms are commonly small and seen to need protection against unfair terms. Thus, terms imposed on consumers and 'small businesses' purporting to limit or exclude the other's liability for breach of contract or carry out the contract in a different way, or not perform at all, are enforceable only if reasonable in the circumstances. S. 3 does not apply when two contracting businesses are not using a standard contract form.

(iii) **Indemnity clauses.** S. 4 provides that a consumer cannot be made to indemnify another for that other's liability for breach of contract or negligence unless reasonable in the circumstances.

(iv) **Manufacturer's guarantees.** S. 5 applies to consumer goods. Guarantees cannot restrict or exclude liability for loss or damage caused by the negligence of the manufacturer or supplier. The protection does not apply to the actual buyer or hire purchasers who have rights under S. 6.

71

(v) **Buyers' and hire purchasers' rights.** S. 6 enacts terms now in the Sale of Goods Act 1979. In 'consumer sales' liability for breach of contract for supplying goods 'not reasonably fit for the purpose intended', or 'not of merchantable quality' cannot be excluded. In 'non-consumer sales' liability under these implied terms can only be excluded in that they pass the test of 'reasonableness'. S. 7 makes similar provisions as to 'fitness for purpose' and 'merchantable quality' for goods hired or provided under a contract for services and not sold or hire-purchased.

(vi) **What is reasonable?** This depends on the facts but the courts consider, inter alia, the relative bargaining strength of the parties; whether other sources are available; whether the customer received any inducement, e.g. lower price for greater risk. The burden of proving that a term satisfies the test of reasonableness attaches to the party putting it forward (often the supplier).

> *Photoproductions Ltd. v. Securicor (1980).* The events here preceded UCTA but the approach of 'reasonableness' was adopted. The patrolman's deliberately lit fire went out of control causing £615,000 damage. According to an exemption, S were 'under no circumstances liable for injurious act or default by any employee unless such act could have been foreseen and avoided by due diligence on the part of the employers, S'. Also they were 'not responsible for any loss . . . by P through fire or any other cause . . . solely attributable to the negligence of S's employees'. It has already been noted that the House of Lords stated the parties were free to use an exemption clause that applied to fundamental breach (although each case depends on construction of the contract as a whole). It was held that the present exemption clause was clear and exempted S. The court also took into account that when the parties have equal bargaining strength and the risks are normally borne by insurance, the parties should be free to apportion risks as they think fit. In the present case P had paid a modest fee and may therefore have expected to carry greater risks.

11.8   **Standard form contracts.** The following examples should be noted:

(a)   **Standard Form of Building Contract** published by the Joint Contracts Tribunal contains:

(i) *Clause 20.1.* The Contractor indemnifies the Employer (Principal in the terms of earlier narrative) for personal injury claims unless the Contractor can show that they were caused by the Employer's negligence. There is no limit as to the amount of this indemnity.

(ii) *Clause 20.2.* Except for certain loss or damage (e.g. damage to the contract works) which **may** be at the sole risk of the Employer, the Contractor must indemnify the Employer against property damage claims provided that it is due to the negligence of the Contractor or his subcontractors. Note that the onus of proof is on the Employer and there may be instances of property damage where there has been no negligence by, or on behalf of the Contractor.

As the above indemnity clauses are confined to negligence and, since sub-contractors can be called upon to give the same indemnity, the main Contractor's position is not made especially onerous.

(iii) *Clause 21.1* is an 'insuring clause' which obliges the contractor to insure his liabilities under 20.1 and 20.2. This is intended to ensure that the Contractor will be able to meet his obligations. Clause 21.1 does not require the insurance to indemnify the Employer directly.

(iv) *Clause 21.2* (formerly 19.2(a)) results from *Gold v. Patman & Fotheringham (1958)*. G of Centrovintial Estates Ltd. awarded P & F a redevelopment contract involving Georgian properties. The work resulted in both adjoining properties being damaged. The developers were liable (nuisance) and expected an indemnity from the contractors, P & F who, not having been negligent, denied liability. The unindemnified developer settled the claims. The intention of 21.2 is to close the gap by securing, for the benefit of the Employer, 'non-negligent' third party cover. The clause is one of insurance and not indemnity with the Contractor arranging the insurance for the Employer. The insurance has to be in joint names but for the benefit only of the Employer, although the Contractor is liable for the premiums and is responsible for complying with warranties. The insurance has to cover both the liability of the Employer and damage to property (excluding the contract works), thus including some 'own damage' risks as well as third party property. The indemnity limit is left to be stated in the contract bills. The cover is against 'nuisance perils' only, e.g. collapse, subsidence, vibration, weakening/removal of support, lowering of ground water. Negligence of Contractors and sub-contractors (covered under public liability insurance) is excepted. The clause applies whenever a provisional sum is included in the bills or specification. The clause is more likely to be invoked by an Employer when the work affects adjoining property than one whose work is in an isolated spot.

Contractors' Plant-hire Association Conditions (C.P.A.). Mechanical plant is often hired out by owners to civil engineers, contractors, and others in the construction industry. The C.P.A. Model Conditions for Hiring Plant (Sept. 1979) resulted from negotiations between C.P.A. (plant hire industry), the Federation of Civil Engineering Contractors (main client industry), and the Office of Fair Trading. Important conditions are:

(i) **Condition 4** makes the hirer responsible for personnel lent by the owner and involved in loading and unloading operations. The clause appears to be one of indemnity as regards third party claims and, when the customer is a non-consumer, as is usually the case, it will be unaffected by UCTA. If the customer is a consumer, S. 4 UCTA applies and makes the clause subject to the test of reasonableness.

(ii) **Condition 8** by which the owner undertakes to supply a competent operator/driver with control vested in the hirer whose servants or agents they become for all purposes connected with the employment. The hirer is made responsible for all claims from the operation of the plant by the driver/operator. The owner appears to be relieved of his employers and public liability risks. The remarks of (i) above regarding UCTA apply, but as Clause 8 also makes the hirer responsible for loss/damage to the plant, it becomes an exemption clause in regard to such loss or damage, and therefore subject to the test of reasonableness.

(iii) **Conditon 13 — Hirers' responsibility for loss or damage.** This makes the hirer responsible for loss/damage to the plant and for third party claims without affecting Condition 8. The owner accepts liability for loss/damage/injury in certain circumstances, e.g. prior to delivery to site.

Note — In *Arthur White (Contractors) v. Tarmac Civil Engineering Ltd. (1967)*, a site engineer was injured after the operator left the boom at 45 degrees instead of lowering it. The owners were partly responsible for this failure but under C.P.A. conditions 8 and 13 full responsibility shifted to the hirer.

CHAPTER 12

PRINCIPLES OF INSURANCE

It is important to have a good grasp of the principles of insurance and be able to apply them to liability insurance.

1. INSURABLE INTEREST

12.1   Insurable interest means having a financial involvement. As a party is prejudiced by having to pay compensation to another and/or incurring costs defending allegations, and would benefit by the absence of such liability or allegations, the potential liabilities are insurable. The essentials of insurable interest in liability insurance are:

(a)   There must be potential liability.

(b)   The legal liability must be the subject-matter of insurance.

(c)   The insured must be prejudiced by the creation or allegation of liability.

12.2   **Time of insurable interest.** Interest must exist at both inception of the contract and time of loss.

12.3   **Insurance covering other interests.** A man has no insurable interest in the liability of others but can insure them as agent provided the principal authorises or ratifies the insurance. Also a person can constitute himself as a trustee for a third party and confer the benefits of the insurance on that third party. It is not a requirement that the agent or trustee should have an interest. There are many instances in liability insurance of the insured extending his policy to indemnify other parties as reference to the main policies will show. In personal liability, cover featured as an extension of a householder's contents policy, the insured effects insurance on behalf of members of his family residing with him despite having no interest in the possible personal liability they may incur. Motor insurance is no longer a part of this text but perhaps it should be mentioned that S. 148(4) Road Traffic Act creates a statutory contract between the insurer and a driver specified as a person indemnified under the insurance.

12.4 Liability caused by criminal acts. The rule 'ex turpi causa non oritur actio' prevents the criminal from recovering under his liability policy. However, the victim's interests may still be protected. In *Hardy v. M.I.B. (1964)* a security guard tried to stop a car bearing a stolen road fund licence. The driver, who was uninsured, drove on injuring the guard. The Road Traffic Act conferred on the victim a direct right of action against the insurer. In *Haseldine v. Hoskin (1938)* a solicitor was unable to recover following an intentional criminal act. But a recovery can be made for mere acts of negligence even though criminal. In *Tinline v. White Cross (1921)* an insured recovered under a motor policy even though guilty of man-slaughter. However, where an insured knowlingly uses a lethal weapon to frighten or harm a third party, it is against public policy to permit a recovery under a liability policy *(Gray v. Barr (1971))*. A person can never insure against liability to pay fines after convictions.

2. INDEMNITY

12.5 This means, subject to the limits of the policy, giving an exact financial compensation. In liability insurance, where the insured's loss is expressed in financial terms, it is possible to give the perfect indemnity. In property insurance estimates may have to be made. However, inadequate indemnity limits may deprive the insured of a full indemnity. Where the limit is an aggregate sum for the period of insurance, reinstatement of the original sum is possible to restore the full sum after claims have been paid. Under most policies the insured's own costs are payable in addition to the limit of indemnity. Under E.L. insurance the indemnity is unlimited.

3. SUBROGATION

12.6 This is a corollary of indemnity and is the right of an insurer, who has paid for a loss, to take over the insured's alternative rights and remedies against any third party liable for the loss. As tort often provides the means by which a property insurer recovers his loss (e.g. fire insurer pursues a claim against a negligent contractor) liability insurers may find themselves the ultimate recipients of the loss. Nonetheless there are circumstances in which the liability insurer can exercise subrogation rights against others. Examples:

(a) **Tort** — one of several concurrent tortfeasors may be held liable. His insurer may, in the name of the insured, pursue a contribution from other tortfeasors.

(b) **Contract.** A vendor of a defective product may have secured an indemnity agreement from the supplier for liability arising from the product. The vendor's liability insurer may then enforce the indemnity. Where a principal is indemnified by a contractor for legal liability to the contractor's employees, the principal's public liability insurer will generally be able to shift the responsibility to the contractor under contractual arrangements. Where the customary principal's clause applies this in effect moves the loss to the contractor's E.L. insurer.

(c)   **Statute.** A bailee may have accepted liability for certain damage (e.g. fire) to bailors' property under contract. In the event of fire damage caused by riot, the bailee's insurer will be able to exercise subrogation rights against the relevant police authority under the Riot (Damages) Act 1886. Also, the chain of supply situation in products cases may create recovery rights against an earlier supplier (this overlaps with contract).

    N.B. An E.L. insurer, meeting a liability where the insured's liability attached because of the provisions of the Employers Liability (Defective Equipment) Act 1969, may have subrogation rights against the manufacturer or supplier of the equipment. Those rights may arise under tort, contract, or statute.

12.7 Subrogation rights waived or denied

(a)   **E.L. cases.** Employers held vicariously liable for injury caused by one worker to another waive their subrogation rights against the negligent employees.

(b)   **Subrogation rights denied when inequitable.** The Court of Appeal refused subrogation in *Morris v. Ford Motor Co. (1973)*. C Industrial Services were contracted to clean at Ford's who required C to indemnify them in respect of F's liability for the negligence of either of them. F became liable when their employee injured Morris and sought an indemnity from C. C's position was analogous to that of an insurer and so proceeded to make a recovery from F's employee. This recovery was denied as risks of this sort in the employment field ought not to fall on individual employees.

12.8 Subrogation condition. At common law the insurer is not permitted to exercise subrogation rights until after the indemnity payment. However, policies modify the situation enabling insurers to proceed in the name of the insured before the indemnity payment. Also insurers reserve the right of conduct and control of claims.

4. CONTRIBUTION

12.9 This corollary of indemnity applies when, under a contract of indemnity, two or more insurers are liable for the same loss. At common law the insurer is called upon to settle the claim in full and then recover rateable proportion(s) from the other insurers concerned. Normally a policy condition modifies this so that the insured must limit his claim against any one insurer to their proportion of the loss. This obliges the insured to make separate claims against each insurer and is a requirement unlikely to be enforced in practice.

12.10 Essential of contribution. These are:

(a)   There must be two more indemnity contracts in force;

(b)   covering the same interest,

(c)   the same subject-matter,

(d)   against the same peril.

12.11 Examples of contribution. The number of instances in liability insurance is controlled by the use of exclusions where more suitable policies exist. Also the careful definition of 'employees' under P.L. and E.L. policies avoids liability to the parties defined being the subject of indemnity under both policies. Overlaps can occur. A golfer may insure against liability from golfing accidents to find that he has such cover under personal liability insurance.

12.12 Apportionment among insurers. The independent liability method is used. In *Commercial Union v. Hayden (1977)*, CU's liability policy had a limit of £100,000 any one accident. Lloyd's had issued a policy with a £10,000 limit and both policies covered a £4,400 loss. Lloyd's sought an apportionment based on 10:1 ratio having regard to the maximum limits of indemnity. This was rejected. In liability insurance (and others in some circumstances):

(a)   each insurer calculates what they would have been liable for on an independent basis as if the other policy did not exist. Applied — CU's liability £4,400; Lloyd's liability £4,400 as in neither case was the limit exceeded.

(b)   The independent liabilities are aggregated and each insurer's independent liability expressed as a proportion of their liabilities in aggregate. In each case this produces £4,400/£8,800 making each insurer liable for £2,200.

This is more equitable than applying the 10:1 ratio as (i) premiums are not calculated pro rata according to policy limits — the CU's premium was £6 and Lloyd's received £5 for the same cover; (ii) most liability claims fall within a low limit.

The reader should work through the method once more assuming that the above claim exceeded the £10,000 limit of the Lloyd's policy but not the limit of the CU policy.

12.13 Conditions removing contribution. When cover is extended to indemnify parties other than the insured, the insurer often makes the extension inoperative if the party concerned is indemnified under another policy.

5.   UTMOST GOOD FAITH

12.14 The duty is to disclose all material facts. The duty is breached by failure to disclose or misrepresentation rendering the policy voidable ab initio at the option of the aggrieved party. The duty exists independently of the proposal form so a proposer is not permitted to remain silent about material matters not touched upon in the form. Despite compulsory insurance, E.L. insurers can still dispute cover on grounds of non-disclosure.

12.15 Examples of material facts in liability insurance

(a) **Criminal history.** It is hard to generalise but possibly a more lenient view might be taken than in other forms of insurance. The more relevant the conviction and the more serious the penalty the more likely it is that it becomes a material fact. Certainly convictions under the Consumer Safety Act 1978 will be relevant in products liability cover unless old and trivial. Some convictions are 'spent' under the Rehabilitation of Offenders Act 1974 and do not have to be disclosed.

(b) **Accident/claims history.**

(c) **'Occurrences pending'.** This will always be important but assumes special significance in the context of 'claims-made' policies.

(d) **Contractual liability.** Even though policies may not exclude contractual liability, the insured should disclose matters relevant thereto except possibly in those parts of the building trade where the contractual liability is the rule and not the exception.

(e) **American exposures.** These will always be material.

(f) **Discontinued activities or products.** Where retrospective cover is arranged the insured should supply details not only to comply with the disclosure requirement but also to ensure that the Business is correctly described.

(g) **Waiver of subrogation rights.**

12.16 Proposal form and declaration. The effect is to convert statements into warranties in the usual way. In the case of larger P.L. and E.L. risks, survey reports may supplement or replace proposal forms. The insured cannot be held responsible for failing to disclose matters which should have been evident to the surveyor.

12.17 Duration of the duty to disclose. The duty is pre-contractual but revives, in the case of annual contracts, at renewal. In the absence of policy conditions there is no need to disclose changes during the currency of the policy. It is customary to find a 'change of risk' clause in a products liability policy so a manufacturer who changes his method will need to give notice at the time of change.

6. PROXIMATE CAUSE

12.18 The definition in *Pawsey v. Scottish Union (1907)* should be memorised — 'the active efficient cause that sets in motion a train of events without the intervention of any other force started and working actively from a new and independent source'.

12.19 Competing causes. Examination questions often involve problems where there are two competing causes, one of which is insured and the other excepted. The following approach is suggested:

(a) First identify and specify the competing causes;

(b) Enquire — do they arise in sequence or are they concurrent causes?

(c) Does the original cause predominate or merely facilitate a later cause?

79

(d)   If the sequence of events is unbroken which comes first, the insured peril or the excepted peril?

(e)   If the sequence is broken, at what point do the effects of the insured peril commence or run out?

(f)   If the causes are concurrent, can the effects be separated?

Remember in all cases, the accident facilitating the loss must be distinguished from the accident causing the loss; and losses from attempts to mitigate the loss are part of the loss.

12.20 Competing causes in *Wayne Tank & Pump Co. v. Employers Liability (1974)*

WT, having failed to benefit from an exemption clause, sought an indemnity from their insurers whose P.L. policy covered negligence (an insured peril) but excluded liability arising from defective products. Defective equipment was installed in a factory but WT's employee negligently switched on the equipment and left it overnight. The resultant fire gutted the factory.

The competing causes: negligence (insured), defective product (excepted).

Did the original cause predominate? The defective equipment was the original cause and was not a spent force so that the subsequent negligence did not totally alter the situation. On this approach the sequence of events is unbroken starting from defective equipment (an excepted peril) so the liability for the damage is not covered. The Court of Appeal in rejecting WT's claim adopted this approach. If neither cause had predominated, i.e. given concurrent causes, the effects of which cannot be separated, the insurer is entitled to the benefit of the exception. In this instance, whichever approach is adopted, the exception applies.

CHAPTER 13

EMPLOYERS LIABILITY INSURANCE

1. EMPLOYERS LIABILITY (COMPULSORY INSURANCE) ACT

13.1   The desire to ensure that injured workmen are not denied their rightful compensation for want of funds, has led to employers liability insurance becoming compulsory.

13.2   **Employers Liability (Compulsory Insurance) Act 1969** makes this insurance compulsory and obliges insurers to issue policies and certificates. The policy must be 'approved'. There is no obligation to insure liability to certain relatives and nationalised industries, certain local and police authorities are exempt.

13.3   **Approved policies.** The insurer issuing the policy must be authorised. The limit of indemnity must be a minimum of £2m. any one occurrence. Regulations prohibit reliance by the insurer on certain conditions; these are conditions precedent to liability relating to matters of claims notification and conduct, reasonable care, compliance with enactments, and the keeping of records. The prohibition is only for the purposes of the Act and helps secure the position of the victim, but the insurer whose payment is due to the prohibition has a right of recovery against the insured.

2. EMPLOYERS LIABILITY INSURANCE COVER

13.4   Liability insurance is often purchased in the form of a combined policy in which the traditional policies can be identified. Certainly for purposes of study there are advantages in dealing with each liability risk separately and considering the policy cover relevant thereto. The approach adopted is to consider in each case the main cover, the extensions and exclusions.

13.5   **Main policy provisions**

(a)   **The indemnity.** The insured is indemnified in respect of legal liability for damages to employees in respect of bodily injury or disease caused during the period of insurance and arising out of and in the course of employment by the insured in the Business. The indemnity is unlimited in amount and goes on to include:

   (i)   claimant's costs and the insured's own costs if incurred with the insurer's consent.

   (ii)   solicitor's fees for representation (a) at any Coroner's inquest or fatal accident enquiry or (b) defending any proceedings in a Court of Summary Jurisdiction where the death or proceedings relate to acts or omissions which may be the subject of indemnity under the policy.

   (iii)   indemnity, in the event of the insured's death, to his personal representatives.

(iv) **Territorial limits.** It may state that the policy does not apply to injury or disease caused elsewhere than in Gt. Britain, N. Ireland, the Isle of Man, the Channel Islands and offshore installations around Gt. Britain and its continental shelf. The restriction does not apply to employees temporarily employed elsewhere if they normally reside in the territories stated. (Alternatively it may state that the contract of employment was made in the U.K. Some insurers restrict cover outside these territories to non-manual workers while another feature of the overseas cover may be the inclusion of a specific **jurisdiction clause**. The purpose of the clause is to ensure that cover is restricted to claims being brought in U.K. courts.) Some policies now describe the territories in E.E.C. terms and this tendency is likely to increase.

(v) (i) **Extended definitions.** The term **Business** is important as the policy applies only to the Business defined in the policy. Business is stated to include:

(a) canteens, sports, social and welfare organisations run for the employees and fire, security, first-aid and ambulance services.

(b) private work carried out by an employee for any director, partner or senior employee.

(c) ownership, maintenance and repair of premises used in connection with the Business.

(ii) **Employees** are 'persons under a contract of service or apprenticeship with the insured' but to overcome problems of workpeople whose status is difficult to determine and who might for some purposes be regarded as independent contractors, a wider definition is used. The extended definition covers:

- any labour masters or labour only sub-contractors or persons supplied by them.
- self-employed persons.
- persons hired or borrowed by the insured.
- persons undergoing work experience schemes.

Main policy provision-points to consider:

(a) **Legal liability** is wide enough to embrace liability arising out of common law, contract and statute. There is no claim by the employee in the absence of legal liability although the insurer may consent to costs incurred in defending claims that prove groundless.

(b) **Bodily injury or disease.** No form of property is covered but when clothing damage accompanies injury, for which there is legal liability, the E.L. insurer normally pays.

(c) **Caused during the period of insurance.** The policy is on a 'losses-occurring basis' (or 'damage-occurring'). Thus, in latent injury cases (e.g. asbestosis — 'a long-tail' case) it is the time of injury not its discovery, which could be many years later, which determines the liability of the insurer. If on risk when the injury occurred it is irrelevant that the policy had lapsed by the time of discovery. The compulsory insurance legislation precludes the use of the claims-made form in E.L. insurance.

(d)   **Arising out of and in the course of employment.** Injury unconnected with the work, albeit to an employee (as defined), is for the public liability insurer. The difficulties, to which reference should be made, regarding motor journeys to or from work were noted in para. 7.11.

13.6   **Main policy extensions**

(a)   *Health & Safety at Work Act 1974* **(legal defence costs)**
In addition to the costs covered in the main indemnity cover is available to the insured, any partner or director, or employee in connection with costs of legal representation upon a criminal prosecution brought under the Act if relating to the health and safety of employees. Some insurers restrict the cover to cases where an employee's claim is the subject of the main indemnity but usually the cover operates regardless of injury to employees. The policy does not cover fines or penalties nor does it cover deliberate acts or omissions but the offence must occur during the period of insurance and arise out of the employment of the person prosecuted.

(b)   **Unsatisfied court judgments.** Employees may have unsatisfied judgments against U.K. based parties for injury sustained in the course of employment. Subject to the terms of the policy, the insurer will meet the payment of compensation.

(c)   **Retrospective cover** is available from some insurers. Given that some diseases (e.g. asbestosis, occupational deafness) have a 'long-tail' and the policy is on a 'losses-occurring basis', the insured may not be able to identify insurers who carried the risk at an earlier time (possibly many years). The possibility of an uninsured loss for at least a proportion of the loss arises. The purpose of the extension is to bring this type of loss within the policy.

((d)   **Indemnity to other parties.** At the insured's request, the insurer will indemnify the officers, committee members, and members of the sports and social organisations etc. described in the 'extended definition'. Partners, directors and employees too are covered (each party being treated as though individually named as the insured).

(e)   **A 'principal's clause'** is usually included protecting principals of the insured in respect of liability for which the insured would have been entitled to seek indemnity if the claim had been made against him. Some insurers stipulate that the cover operates only when required by the insured's contract or agreement with the principal. The principal's indemnity is subject to the radioactivity exclusion (see below). The insurer retains conduct and control of all claims.

The parties indemnified ((d) and (e) above) must observe the terms and conditions of the policy.

13.7   **Policy exclusions.** The only exclusion (apart from the restrictions within the operative clause) relates to liability for radioactive contamination or nuclear assembly risks where the liability is (a) that of any principal; (b) assumed by the insured under agreement and would not otherwise have attached.

However, exclusions of particular work may be introduced by trade endorsements. For example the more hazardous risks of the building trade may be excluded in this way for those tradesmen whose activities are of a more limited nature. In this way they are prevented from subsidising others who run and pay for the greater risks. In *Kearney v. General Accident (1968)*, the insured was unable to recover as the accident occurred at premises coming within the description of excluded places of work in that it exceeded 25 ft. in height. The use of such restrictions by insurers is not constrained by the compulsory insurance legislation *(Dunbar v. A. & B. Painters, Economic Insurance and Another (1986))*.

3. LEGAL EXPENSES INSURANCE

13.8   This form of insurance, as noted, features in some respects as an extension of the E.L. policy. It has become a separate and more extended form of insurance in its own right. Insurance is sought by individuals and businesses who face the risk of incurring legal expenses either because of actions against them or because of actions they need to bring against others. Legal rights are often not pursued because the legal costs may outweigh the value of any awards; costs are a barrier where the outcome is uncertain; legal aid may not be available and yet resources limited; the opponent may be more financially capable.

Modular approach. Commercial cover is typically provided for businesses under seven sections but cover is not available for motor vehicle aspects (separate insurance exists). The choice of cover is:

(a)   Contract of employment cover.

(b)   Prosecution defence cover.

(c)   Contract cover.

(d)   Property legal protection cover.

(e)   Employees protection.

(f)   Inland Revenue/VAT cover.

(g)   Employment Awards Cover.

The limit of indemnity is typically £50,000 per incident but there are variations.

The cover is for legal fees and associated expenses incurred by the insured in defending legal rights and prosecutions and, under appropriate sections, pursuing legal rights against others (e.g. enforcement of judgment debts). In civil cases the insurer's pay the third party costs if they fall upon the insured. In criminal cases fines and prosecution costs are not covered. Cover is available for individuals and families in much the same way.

CHAPTER 14

PUBLIC LIABILITY INSURANCE

14.1 This form of policy covers legal liability for bodily injury (to other than employees) and loss/damage to the property of third parties. An important exception is that of product liability. Primarily the policy covers the risks of premises and activities.

14.2 Main policy provisions

(a) **The indemnity.** The insured is indemnified against legal liability to pay damages for accidental bodily injury to any person and accidental loss or damage to material property occurring during the period of insurance in connection with the Business. Some policies do not qualify the injury/damage aspects with 'accidental' but as they proceed to exclude 'inevitable' damage the net effect is much the same. The insured benefits from this approach by not being called upon to show that the injury/damage was accidental and it is for the insurer to bring any particular case within the scope of an exclusion. Some insurers additionally cover accidental nuisance, trespass, obstruction or interference with any right of way, light, air or water leading to financial loss. Also some cover liability from such risks as wrongful arrest and invasion of right of privacy.

The indemnity extends to:

(i) claimant's costs and the insured's own costs if incurred with the insurer's consent.

(ii) solicitors' fees for representation (a) at any Coroner's inquest or fatal enquiry or (b) defending any proceedings in a Court of Summary Jurisdiction where the death or proceedings relate to acts or omissions which may be the subject of indemnity under the policy.

(iii) indemnify, in the event of the insured's death, his personal representatives.

(b) **Territorial limits** normally restrict cover to injury/damage occurring within the U.K. (as in the E.L. policy) and, increasingly, the E.E.C. Cover also applies elsewhere in the world arising from non-manual activities of members of the Business normally resident within the stated territories during journeys or temporary visits. Insurers may insist upon U.K. jurisdiction, the complexities of which are illustrated in *Berliner Motor Corporation & Anr. v. Sun Alliance & London (1983)*.

(c) **Limit of indemnity.** Insurers limit their liability in regard to the amount payable as compensation and claimants' costs in respect of any one occurrence or all occurrences consequent upon, or attributable to, one source or original cause. Costs and expenses incurred with the insurer's consent are payable in addition. Annual limits may be introduced when special risks are covered (e.g. weakening of support accorded to buildings (building trade)), otherwise there is no limit in regard to the period of insurance.

(d) **Extended definitions**

   (i) **The Business** — as per the E.L. policy but extended further to give personal liability cover when members of the Business journey or visit (temporarily) outside the territorial limits.

   (ii) **Employees** — as per E.L. policy. Liability for injury to employees is excluded and it is important that they should be defined in the same terms as in the E.L. policy so that the relevant policy can be readily identified.

Main policy provision — points to consider:

(a) **Legal liability** and, as in E.L., not moral liability, is the basis and is itself wide in scope.

(b) **Losses-occurring basis** remains the traditional basis on which cover is provided although the 'hard market' situation of 1985/6 saw a move towards 'claims-made' policies.

(c) **Single occurrence limit** is expressed in the manner shown to avoid problems arising in 'multi-claimant situations'. e.g. If a football stand collapsed due to a breach of duty causing injury to 40 spectators it could be argued that each injury constituted a separate occurrence leaving the limit to be applied separately in the case of each claimant. The insurer may regard the collapse as the single occurrence and apply the limit of indemnity to the aggregate of all claims arising. The wording makes it clear that the limit imposes a ceiling to all claims due to the collapse. This is not unfair as the insured exposed to risk in this way should seek to insure for a limit high enough to safeguard himself against multiple-claims and catastrophies.

14.3 Main policy extensions

(a) **Legal expenses** cover is required in respect of offences under the Health & Safety at Work Act 1974 as the E.L. extension is confined to matters involving safety of employees. The extension applies when the public liability risk is covered and proceedings relate to any person other than an employee.

(b) **Retrospective cover,** when the extension applies, makes the insurer liable for claims made during the period of insurance notwithstanding that the damage/injury occurred prior to inception. Thus, a 'claims-made' situation is grafted on to a 'losses-occurring' policy. There must be no claim under another policy. The intention is to close gaps that can arise in latent injury/damage cases which produce late claims (e.g. pollution). Gaps may arise because previous insurers cannot be traced.

(c) **Indemnity to other parties.** Officers, committee members and other members of canteens, social organisation etc. Partners, directors, and employees, each party being treated as though individually insured.

(d) **Cross liabilities clause** provides that where there is more than one party named as the Insured each will be treated as though separately insured. The liability to all parties is limited in aggregate to the limit of indemnity.

(e) **Principal's clause.** This extension is a standard feature in so far as it indemnifies the principal of the insured against liability in respect of which the insured would have, had the claim been made against him, been entitled to indemnity. Under some policy wordings the extension applies only when the insured's contract with the principal calls for the benefit of the policy. The insurer retains sole conduct and control of claims and principals who wish to have it otherwise may have to forego the benefit of the policy.

(f) **Motor vehicles — contingent liability.** The insured is exposed to certain risks in connection with non-owned vehicles, e.g. when an employee uses his own car on his employer's business, the latter secures an indemnity under the employee's private car policy. If the policy fails (because of breach of condition or duty of disclosure) the employer is exposed to the risk of an uninsured loss. This extension indemnifies the insured in the event that liability attaches but is not met by the employee's policy. The extension would also benefit the insured when hiring-in a car with driver in reliance on the owner's primary insurance.

(g) **Tool of trade risk.** Mechanical plant, e.g. bulldozers, excavators, may be insured under motor policies but it may be necessary to extend the P.L. policy to cover damage while the plant is used as a tool of trade to cover such instances as damage to underground cables and other 'on-site accidents'.

(h) **Defective Premises Act 1972.** As a result of S. 3, the owner may now be liable for pre-disposal negligence even after disposing of the premises. The policy is extended but the insurer excludes liability for the cost of remedying any defect. The purpose is to cover the resultant losses.

(i) **Financial loss.** Not all insurers are prepared to provide this extension and, following the very narrow application of *Junior Books v. Veitchi*, the demand is also limited. Such an extension is more likely to be associated with products cover but, given the uncertainty on some occasions of the dividing line between the two covers, it is wise to extend the P.L. policy when the products cover has been extended. The purpose of the extension is to cover accidental financial loss not occasioned by physical loss or damage to property caused otherwise than by goods sold or supplied. The extra protection may be arranged on a 'claims-made' basis, be the subject of a lower limit of indemnity, subject to co-insurance, exclusion of contractual liability, exclusion of breach of professional duty, infringement of copyrights or patents, etc.

14.4 **Main policy exclusions.** Exclusions fall under three headings: Risks more suitably insured under another policy; risks needing individual attention; uninsurable risks.

14.5 **Injury to employees.** Separately insured (E.L. risk).

14.6 **Motor vehicle risks.** Wordings vary. It is a minimum to exclude vehicles licensed for road use in circumstances to which the Road Traffic Act compulsory insurance requirements apply. Also there is no cover if a more specific insurance exists. Cover should remain in tact for unlicensed vehicles when used on private property such as sites. The exclusion should be so drawn that it does not apply to unloading/loading activities that are not covered under the commercial motor policy.

14.7 **Aircraft and waterborne craft.** These are normally matters for the marine and aviation department. The exclusion is frequently overridden in the matter of small craft and the contingent or vicarious liability arising from the use of the craft of others.

14.8 **Goods sold, supplied, repaired, serviced etc.** Risks of this type are the subject of products liability insurance. The term 'goods' includes containers and wrapping. The exclusion is overridden in the cases of:

(a) food and drink sold for consumption on the insured premises (thus restaurants etc. do not have to effect separate products cover);

(b) goods still in the insured's possession (this creates an important dividing line between the products and P.L. insurances. Even though an accident is technically a product defect case, if that product is still in the insured's possession it is treated as a P.L. risk. Even where the insurances are with the same insurer (and they should be to avoid gaps) this is important because the policies are governed by different terms (e.g. different approaches on indemnity lmits and different exclusions).

14.9 **Advice or treatment.** The intention is to exclude the risks which are insurable under professional indemnity insurance. This is often achieved by excluding advice given by the insured for a fee or in circumstances where a fee would normally be charged. If the exclusion is treated in this way 'non-professional' advice leading to injury/damage (as described) is covered. Advice often forms an integral feature of many businesses in situations which fall well short of the circumstances which are covered by professional indemnity insurances. An absolute exclusion of all advice could therefore create problems. The 'treatment' exclusion ensures that members of the medical profession do not secure professional indemnity cover at inappropriate rates but the exclusion is made inapplicable to first-aid treatment.

14.10 **Property in the insured's custody and control** is excluded as material damage policies may be more appropriate. One of the chief effects if to exclude the bailment risk (e.g. dry-cleaners). However, rigorous application of the exclusion would produce unfortunate results. Consequently it is now usual to override the exclusion in the following instances:

(a) the personal effects or vehicles of any partner, director, or employee of, or visitor to, the insured.

(b) premises (and their contents) not belonging, leased, rented or hired to the insured but temporarily in the insured's charge for the purpose of carrying out work. (This is an important provision for members of the building trade.)

(c)   premises (including fixtures and fittings) leased, rented, or hired to, the insured but excluding liability that attaches solely under the terms of any tenancy or other agreement. An excess of £100 is commonly applied.

14.11 Property being worked upon. Some insurers specifically exclude damage to that part of the property the insured has been working on. It is not the insurer's function to guarantee the standard of workmanship but only to insure the consequences of defective workmanship. A house may be destroyed by fire following the careless use of a painter's blowlamp on a window-frame. The house destruction would be covered minus the cost of damage to the window-frame. The effect is to exclude a form of loss and not a risk.

14.12 Contract Works and JCT (RIBA) Clause 21.2.1. This is relevant to the construction industry and refers to the need to make special arrangements for the insurance on the works itself and the obligation on the contractor to insure for the benefit of the principal under the stated clause (see para. 11.8(a)(iv)). As noted, the cover for 21.2.1 makes provision for the effecting of 'non-negligent' cover for the benefit of the Employer with the cover being required only when specified in the contract documents. The task of arranging the insurance is that of the contractor. The special policy covers:

(a)   the liability of the Employer and damage to his own property (other than the contract works).

(b)   'non-negligent' insurance i.e. against 'nuisance perils', e.g. damage to property caused by collapse, subsidence, etc.

(c)   only the Employer but is in the joint names of Employer and Contractor.

The indemnity is for any one event or any one period with a sizeable excess. Negligence of the contractor is excepted. Other exceptions — design risks; reasonably foreseeable damage having regard to the nature of the work.

14.13 Subsidence, collapse or removal or weakening of support. Insurers providing cover for the building trade do not include this exception but introduce a lower limit of indemnity while also applying an excess.

14.14 Pollution is a risk sometimes excluded but restriction may be imposed in particular cases as an underwriting measure. In any event the extent of the protection depends on the operative clause so the cover applies only when the injury/damage is accidental in origin. Also certain 'interferences' causing financial loss may be covered. (The risk poses particular problems in those cases where there is an American exposure as cover in that context is not readily available.)

14.15 Contractual liability. The modern tendency is to exclude liability for liquidated damages or penalties that attach solely out of a contract or agreement. These risks are virtually uninsurable. However, although contractual liability is not otherwise excluded, the insured should appreciate that his cover remains subject to the terms and conditions of the policy. This may well leave him with certain contractual liabilities uninsured or inadequately insured giving rise to the need for discussions and negotiations with the insurer.

14.16 **War and kindred risks** are excluded by way of a market agreement.

14.17 **Radioactive contamination and nuclear assemblies**
Legislation places liability on nuclear reactor owners and in some circumstances liability attaches to the government or the Atomic Energy Authority.

PERSONAL LIABILITY INSURANCE

14.17 Legal liability may arise from social and private pursuits which take place in a person's ordinary life (e.g. jaywalking, horse riding, ownership of a pet). Cover is provided generally as a part of a householder's policy. This cover is in broad terms but exceptions remove risks more suitably insured under other policies. The indemnity is for the insured and members of his family normally residing with him.

14.19 **Exceptions** refer to motor vehicle risks; marine and aviation; premises; business/occupation; injury to members of the household; employees; property in the insured's custody or control; contractual liability.

14.20 **Unrecovered damage** is an extension to compensate the insured when, as a claimant in circumstances to which this type of cover applies, he has been unable to recover from the third party concerned.

CHAPTER 15

PRODUCTS LIABILITY INSURANCE

15.1   Simple risks can be insured by overriding the relevant exclusion in the P.L. policy. The potential for injury/damage arising from products is considerable and may have its origin in defective manufacture; incorrect use of product; inadequate warning; misleading labelling; wrong delivery etc. The intention of products liability cover is to provide indemnity against liability for such risks.

15.2   **MAIN POLICY PROVISIONS**

(a)   **The indemnity.** The insured is indemnified in respect of legal liability to pay damages and claimants' costs in respect of accidental bodily injury and accidental damage to material property occurring during the period of insurance and caused by or arising out of products supplied, etc. in connection with the Business. Insured's own costs, if consented to by the insurer, are covered as will be solicitors' fees for representation at inquests etc. and courts of summary jurisdiction in the same manner as in the P.L. policy. Also in the event of the insured's death, cover continues for the personal representatives.

    (i)   **Territorial limits.** The injury/damage may happen anywhere in the world elsewhere than at premises owned or occupied by the insured caused by products supplied from the U.K. (Clearly it is important to cover exports and goods purchased by tourists in the U.K., but the supply risk is essentially intended to be a U.K. one. If supply is from overseas, negotiations with the insurer will be necessary and once again the question of jurisdiction arises.)

    (ii)   **Limit of indemnity.** This is stated to be a maximum for any one period of insurance. A single accident or occurrence limit is difficult to apply. What is the occurrence? Is it the original act of negligence or each separate consequence when multiple claims result from a defective batch of goods? Reinstatement of the yearly limit can be arranged after its erosion by a claim. Most insurers apply the limit to damages and claimants' costs with insured's own costs payable in addition. However, if there is an American risk, insured's own costs may be brought within the limit for that part of the risk.

    Points to consider:
- There must be damage or injury to a third party. Failure of the product to perform its intended fucntion resulting in purely financial loss is not covered.
- the policy is 'losses occurring' so the date of manufacture is not relevant. It also follows that the insurer is not liable for damage caused after expiry even though that damage arises from negligence occurring during the currency of the policy.

- if injury or damage occurs on the insured's own premises this is likely to arise from goods still in the insured's possession and is treated as a P.L. risk. The relevant P.L. exclusion should be compared with the wording of the products cover as the dividing line between the two policies is important.
- products are widely defined meaning goods or other property sold, supplied, delivered, installed, erected, repaired, altered, treated, or tested.

15.3   MAIN POLICY EXTENSIONS

(a)   **Legal defence costs.** There is an increasing amount of legislation, including Part II of the Consumer Protection Act 1987, creating criminal offences making this extension a desirable one.

(b)   **Financial loss** cover is an extension to bring within the policy liability for accidental financial loss caused by goods sold or supplied as a direct result of those goods having been defective, harmful or having failed to perform the intended function. There does not have to be any accompanying injury or property damage. The cost of recalling or replacing goods is not covered and a co-insurance clause is introduced together with special exclusions similar to those referred to in para. 14.3. Cover is often arranged on a 'claims-made basis'.

(c)   **Retrospective cover.** The demand for this extension arises from the 'long-tail' potential of some products (e.g. pharmaceuticals). As in other instances, the extension does not operate to overcome restrictions in earlier policies or breaches of conditions, but to fill gaps because of inability to trace the previous insurer.

(d)   **Indemnity to other parties** follows the E.L. and P.L. policies. Further extensions may be necessary on occasions. An insured who has offered to indemnify a vendor of his product may seek an extension to enable him to overcome the obstacles of the contractual liability exclusion.

(e)   **Products guarantee and product recall** are dealt within para. 15.5/6 below.

15.4   MAIN POLICY EXCLUSIONS
Some follow the lines of the P.L. policy, viz: employers liability risk; insured's own property and property in his custody or control; war risks; radio-activity and nuclear assembly.

(a)   **Contractual liability.** The insurer generally excludes liability arising out of agreement that would not otherwise have attached. This limits the risk to that which is ascertainable at common law and by reference to statute. Insureds who vary their liabilities will have to negotiate with the insurer.

(b)   **Replacement of goods.** Replacement, reinstatement, recall, guarantee of performance involve some risks insurable under products guarantee insurance and so are excluded. The exclusion should be made inapplicable to: (i) work executed or goods supplied under a separate contract (e.g. while installing B, A sold and supplied at an earlier date is damaged. Cover for liability for A should remain intact.) (ii) Where an item is one (e.g. a component) of a number of parts and incorporated into another, often highly valued product, the exclusion should be of the part and not the whole product.

(c) **Efficacy clause.** Practice varies where a product fails to perform its intended function. Some insurers exclude all loss/damage arising from the failure. Others, subject to the terms of the policy which does not cover pure financial loss — unless extended, will provide cover subject to the exclusion of loss or damage to the product supplied.

(d) **Advice, design and specification.** The wording varies but cover is generally available for design risks. The intention is to remove from the cover professional negligence risks and the unsuitability of the product which is a matter for products guarantee insurance.

(e) **Liability for goods installed in aircraft or ships.** Practice varies but the aviation market caters for aircraft component manufacturers. The catastrophe potential in any event is such that cover ought not to be given unwittingly and special consideration should be given. However, some insurers are prepared to override the exclusion where the goods to be installed, e.g. soft furnishing, do not affect the safety of the craft.

2. PRODUCTS GUARANTEE INSURANCE

15.5   This covers legal liability to pay damages and claimant's costs in respect of:

(a)   cost of removal, repair, replacement etc. of a defective product or a part thereof that has failed to perform its intended function;

(b)   consequential financial loss arising.

The cover is on a 'claims-made' basis but does not accommodate losses occurring before inception. It is subject to a limit of indemnity that applies to all claims during the period of insurance. Insured's own costs are not subject to the limit. If any contract so requires, a principal's indemnity applies. A measure of co-insurance is customary. The usual exclusions of employers liability risk, war risks, and radioactivity appear in the policy which also excludes recall expenses. A more limited form of cover is available covering the 'replacement' risk only. However, the market overall is very restricted.

15.6 PRODUCT RECALL EXPENSES

The harmful nature of goods may not be discovered until after distribution. Recall costs could be heavy and, following the Consumer Protection Act 1987, recalls are likely to increase. The purpose of product recall is to meet these expenses. The cover operates in connection with goods whose consumption or use may cause a legal liability for the insured. There is no cover for goods recalled solely because of government or local authority intervention. Neither is there cover for products not distributed, misdelivered or misdirected. Cover is normally an extension of products guarantee.

CHAPTER 16

PROFESSIONAL INDEMNITY INSURANCE

16.1   Claims made against persons or firms engaged in professional duties or the provision of such services for alleged negligence continue to increase. The number of claims against the medical profession has doubled in the last three years, a fact the profession attributes to increased claims consciousness rather than falling standards. Physical injury or death is the most likely outcome when there are claims alleging negligence against members of the medical profession. Their cover is arranged through their own mutual organisations (Medical Defence Union and Medical Protection Society) operating under special reinsurance arrangements. The other 'professionals' are more likely, through their negligence, to cause financial loss which may be the result of giving advice or carrying out an activity (e.g. preparing a survey report, drawing up financial statements) and, in some cases, injury/damage may enter into the matter. Solicitors, insurance brokers, and chartered surveyors are directly or indirectly subject to compulsory insurance. The term Error and Omissions (E & O) cover is sometimes used for policies issued to insurance brokers and others (e.g. investment managers) who may not necessarily be qualified by trade or recognised examination.

16.2   How liability arises

(a)   Under contract as a professional person owes a duty of care to his clients.

(b)   In tort to third parties (see *Hedley Byrne v. Heller & Partners (1963)*). As far as clients are concerned the duty exists under both contract and tort. It is also relevant to note that when there is a change in the ownership of a professional practice, the outgoing owners have a run-off liability but under the terms of the sale the incoming owners may accept liability for run-off claims arising. Where an agent is engaged there may be vicarious liability. This arises in any event in regard to employees even when their acts, provided within the course of employment, though are dishonest. (*Lloyd v. Grace Smith & Co. (1912)* see para 5.4.3.)

PROFESSIONAL INDEMNITY POLICY

(a)   **Main provisions**

(i)   *The indemnity.* The insured is indemnified against claims for damages and claimants' costs for breach of professional duty due to negligent act, error or omission made against him during the period of insurance. Key features:
    ● cover is on a 'claims-made' basis but some insurers limit the retrospective cover by excluding claims due to negligence occurring, say two years, before inception. In any event when cover is effected careful enquiries are made as to 'occurrences' pending so giving the insurer the opportunity to exclude the 'occurrences'. In the event

that cover lapses, insurers generally indicate a willingness to treat claims notified within three months as though they had been notified during the period of insurance. This 'discovery period' is not available if the risk has been transferred to another insurer.

● cover extends to include the insured's costs incurred with the insurer's consent but is subject to a form of average. Where the claim exceeds the limit of indemnity, the costs paid will be limited to that proportion of the costs that the limit of indemnity bears to the amount paid.

● the limit of indemnity is a maximum in any one period of insurance and is applied to damages and claimants' costs but not insured's own costs. Reinstatement can be arranged when the selected limit is eroded.

● the policy is strictly one of 'negligence'. A mere breach of warranty is not covered.

● the negligence must have been committed in the conduct of the Business and negligence by predecessors (including employees) is covered.

● cover often applies on a world-wide basis but jurisdiction clauses may be used.

● the policy is generally subject to a sizeable excess.

16.4   Main extensions

(a)   **Libel and slander.** This may be brought into the policy by deleting the exclusion so that the risks become covered subject to the terms and conditions of the policy. Consequently, libel and slander will be covered only when resulting from a breach of duty. Alternatively, subject to the terms, libel and slander of any person may be covered.

(b)   **Breach of warranty of authority.** Professionals often assume the role of agent and, if they exceed their principal's authority, may incur liability to third parties. Cover, by way of extension, can be arranged.

(c)   **Dishonesty, fraudulent, criminal or malicious act or omission of employees or agents.** This can be covered by rendering the relevant exclusion inoperative to claims caused in these ways by employees or agents but the cover is still based on negligence. Some extensions go wider and do not depend upon negligence.

(d)   **Documents.** Cover operates to cover (i) costs incurred in replacing or restoring documents; (ii) legal liability arising from the loss of documents. The loss must occur in transit or in the custody of the insured or of a person to whom the insured has entrusted them.

(e)   **Run-off risk.** As the policy is 'claims-made', an extension is needed to cover the firm on closing down.

16.6   MAIN EXCEPTIONS

(a)   **Libel and slander.** As shown this exclusion can be amended.

(b)   **Dishonesty, etc., of the insured, employees.** This, too, is capable of amendment.

(c) **P.L. risk.** Bodily injury/property damage are excluded unless arising out of professional negligence.

(d) **Circumstances 'known'** to the insured at the inception but not disclosed. Also circumstances notified to previous insurers are excluded.

16.6 MAIN CONDITIONS
The policy contains conditions which call for special comment.

(a) The insurer retains the right to control all claims but undertakes not to exercise subrogation rights against employees unless the erring employee has been convicted of dishonesty.

(b) **The QC Clause.** This provides a form of arbitration. In the event of a dispute between the insured and the insurer as to whether a claim be disputed or contested, the insurer agrees not to contest a claim unless a mutually agreed Queens Counsel advises that there is a reasonable probability of success.

2. LIBEL & SLANDER

16.7 As an alternative to arranging cover by extending the professional indemnity policy, a separate policy can be arranged covering legal liability for damages, claimants' costs, and insured's own costs incurred with consent. The risks covered are:

(a) Libel;

(b) Slander of title to goods;

(c) Infringement of trademark, registered design, copyright etc. from matter contained in specified publications. Withdrawal expenses are also covered.

The insured is a co-insurer usually for 10% and the indemnity limit is fixed for any one period. The main exceptions are:

Claims arising from spite or ill-will; slander of title to goods; actions outside the UK; criminal libel; contractual liability unless otherwise attaching.

3. DIRECTORS & OFFICERS LIABILITY

16.8 Directors and officers of companies are expected to carry out their duties in a professional manner and the policy available to them is a variant of a professional indemnity policy. Personal liability can attach to directors and officers in both criminal and civil matters. Damages and legal expenses can be very heavy. Liquidation is a circumstance that can create a claims situation. The liquidator may discover losses to the company through negligent performance of duties by directors and seek a recovery. Often, but not always, the duties are owed to, and enforceable through the company itself. Personal liability arises at common law and under statute.

16.9   MAIN POLICY PROVISIONS

The cover (for directors and officers whose names have been advised to the insurer and former holders of identified posts) is for legal liability to pay damages and claimants' costs in respect of claims made against the insured during the period of insurance. The claim must arise from breaches of contract, trust or duty, or act, neglect, error, omission, misstatement, misleading statement or breach of warranty of authority (often collectively 'wrongful acts') by the insured in their respective capacities. Key features include:

- the insured's own costs incurred with written consent are covered.
- costs of representation at official investigations are included.
- the indemnity is for any one period and is inclusive of the insured's own costs.
- policies often have two sections, one indemnifying the directors and officers the other indemnifying the company when reimbursing the directors or officers against claims covered in the main indemnity.
- the policy is 'claims-made'.

16.10   Main extensions

These include: Legal expenses; indemnity to personal representatives; discovery period to cover claims first made after non-renewal provided the 'wrongful act' occurred prior to termination of the policy.

16.11   Main exclusions

These include: Dishonesty and fraud but cover operates for successful defences of allegations of fraud or dishonesty; secret profits; public liability and professional indemnity risks; liability arising under guarantee and warranty; an excess applicable to each insured with an overriding limit in respect of any one claim; the reimbursement from the company is excluded in those policies that do not have a company reimbursement section so that if another insurer is involved responsibility shifts to that insurer.

16.12   Main conditions

These include a Queens Counsel clause and a discharge of liability clause.

4.   PROFESSIONAL RISKS AND THE 'INSURABLE PROFESSIONS'

16.13   The demand for professional indemnity insurance continues to increase. The mid 1980's crisis in the liability market was keenly felt in the P.I. sector. The increased 'claims consciousness' has broadened the base from which cover is sought. The reader should review some of the causes of claims in the context of particular professions and services. The following is intended as a brief illustration of the approach:

(a)   **Barristers** may be liable for pre-trial negligence but public policy bars a claim when the negligence arises in the course of advocacy *(Rondel v. Worsley (1967))*.

(b)   **Solicitors** — wrongful advice; error in documents; failure to act timeously.

(c)   **Accountants** — negligence in audit work; wrong advice on financial statements; failure to detect defalcation; negligent advice to third parties.

(d) **Architects and engineers** — errors in plans and specifications; wrong advice; negligent supervision of work; Defective Premises Act liability.

(e) **Insurance Brokers** — failure to effect cover leading to uninsured loss.

(f) **Estate agents and surveyors** — failure to have plans passed by local authority; overlooking defects in property

(g) **Pharmacists** — negligence in selling or dispensing drugs; negligent advice.

SOLUTIONS TO MULTIPLE CHOICE QUESTIONS

Page 16:   1(b)   2(a)   3(c)   4(c)   5(b)

Page 34:   1(c)   2(b)   3(a)   4(b)   5(c)

Page 56:   1(a)   2(b)   3(a)   4(c)   5(a)

CHAPTER 17

ENGINEERING RISKS

17.1　It is no longer the rule for public liability policies to exclude liability arising out of certain specified plant and machinery but statutory obligations calling for regular inspection result in insurance and inspection being available from engineering insurers. These insurers provide cover in the following groups.

17.2　Lifts, hoists and cranes
　　A P.L. insurer, when providing cover, will wish to ensure that arrangements have been made for inspection. The engineering policy covers:

(a)　**Breakdown and extraneous damage.** This is material damage insurance.

(b)　**Inspection.**

(c)　**Maintenance and repair service.** Some engineering insurers provide this type of service.

(d)　**Public liability.** The indemnity is for legal liability to pay compensation, including claimants' costs, to third parties for accidental bodily injury and accidental loss/damage to property. Damage to personal effects in passenger lifts is covered. There is no cover for property belonging to the insured or in his custody or control. The exclusion extends to property being handled by the plant although an extension can be arranged in connection with this risk. Insured's own costs are covered in the usual way and the limit of indemnity applies to any one occurrence.

17.3　Boilers and pressure vessels
　　The principal risk is explosion and statutory inspection requirements apply. Policy cover:

(a)　**Damage** (other than by fire) to the insured plant or to surrounding property belonging to the insured. Once again, material damage cover applies.

(b)　**Public liability cover.** This covers legal liability to third parties for accidental bodily injury or for accidental loss/damage to their property. It also includes liability for damage to property (excluding fire) held by the insured for which he is responsible. The policy is triggered by an explosion or collapse so that liability attaching for third party claims for other reasons is not within the policy. A single occurrence limit applies.

17.4　**Electrical and mechanical plant.** The engineering department provides material damage cover to the plant plus damage to property not belonging to the insured but for which he is responsible. This type of plant was never the subject of an exclusion under the P.L. policy under whose normal terms cover continues to be available.

CHAPTER 18

LIABILITY INSURANCE EXPOSURES & APPLICATIONS

18.1   An awareness is required of the covers required by those, business and otherwise, exposed to liability risks. It is useful to begin by outlining exposure areas in
general terms with the key words operating as a checklist:

(a)   **Premises.** There are few individuals or businesses where ownership and/or
occupation of premises does not give rise to risk. In general P.L. policies the
extended definition of Business makes it clear that matters relating to the
premises are part of the cover. It is from premises that pollution may arise
and enquiry should be made as to heating and lifting activities which leads
to considerations of exposure from boilers and passenger lifts and other
lifting devices. Premises are disposed from time to time and the exposure
continues in respect of predisposal negligence. The occupiers' liability is
specially important in 'public access' risks such as cinemas where the
premium rating may be based on seating capacity. Legal duties exist not only
between occupiers and third parties but also they arise in landlord/tenant
relationships. It has been noted that the 'custody/control' exclusion of a P.L.
policy needs to be overridden in such a manner as to indemnify the tenant
for liability in respect of the building and, likewise, a similar arrangement to
protect tradesmen when working on someone else's premises.

(b)   **Employment.** In the absence of a checklist it would be easy to concentrate
the mind in an examination on the full range of other liability exposures at
the expense of the obvious EL risk. However, the E might also remind us not
only of liability to employees but liability that they might themselves incur.
Employees of the status of 'officers', along with directors, may incur
personal liability arising out of their running of the company. Thus, wherever
there is a limited company there will be an exposure to which the D & O
policy will be relevant.

(c)   **Activities.** This really embraces matters not within the other exposures.
Liability may arise out of activities on or off the premises. This liability arises
while activities are in progress (e.g. working on third party premises) or after
completion as where a contractor leaves behind something inherently
dangerous in his work. The activities might be of a professional nature, e.g.
giving advice or preparing documents. The exposure for those engaged in
manufacture, distribution and marketing of products continues to increase
and for some firms this may represent their greatest exposure. In practice it
is important to have full details of all activities to determine the extent of
liability insurance needs.

(d)   **Contracts.** Again those supplying goods will have an exposure by way of
contract of sale and this may give rise to the need for products cover. There
is also a reminder here of contract disputes and the contentious areas (e.g.
industrial relations, prosecutions etc.) which are within legal expenses
insurance. Contractual liabilities may arise in a variety of ways depending on
the trade or profession concerned (e.g. CPA conditions).

103

(e)   **Engineering.** Risks under this heading can arise on or off the premises as in the latter instance where contractors work off site with cranes and other plant.

This checklist is intended to help in the examination and can be brought to mind by the mnemonic PEACE which spells out the initial letter of each key word in the checklist.

18.2   Miscellaneous Risks

(a)   **Shops.** Depends on type of shop. Premises risk always arises and, in larger shops, lifts or escalators may be present. Sale of Goods Act risk arises. Some shops 'work away'. This may involve delivery, installation or repair. Careful consideration should be given to the activities of a department store where there may be hairdressing salons, restaurants, and shops within shops.

(b)   **Offices.** These may be multi-tenanted. Lifts may be a feature. Type of user may be important.

(c)   **Warehouses.** Lifting appliances, fork lift trucks may feature. If associated with a wharf, the risk of foul berthing (excluded by some insurers) arises. Also there may be loading directly on to ships or third parties' vehicles. Contractual liabilities may arise in regard to plant owners and shipowners.

(d)   **Factories.** Considerations may involve contractual liabilities; products; lifting and mechanical plant; pollution; use and storage of chemicals; fencing of machinery; training of staff; warnings and protective clothing.

(e)   **Builders and Contractors.** Organisations range from jobbing builders to large nationally known companies. Generally public liability exposures include: visitors to the site; third parties working on the site; owner and occupiers of neighbouring property; contractual liability. Demolition, pile driving and work at heights and on special locations (e.g. viaducts, steeples) may feature as special risks. Subsidence, collapse and vibration also have to be considered on some occasions.

Risks of fire and explosion affect virtually all categories and some form of fire precautions clause is commonly applied. Products and professional indemnity risks also arise within some organisations as well as damage to underground property. The EL cover needs to take account of the 'wider definition'. Insurers have to distinguish between the various categories of risk in order to distribute the premium fairly. For the smaller tradesmen special proposals, which are very informative, exist and are worthy of study.

(f)   **Public and local authorities** are singled out because of the diversity and extent of their activities. Liability may have its origin in:

(i)   **Premises** — council houses, offices, public halls, multi-storey car parks, baths, schools, markets, industrial risks.

(ii)   **Professional risks** — solicitors, surveyors, hospitals, school authorities, etc.

(iii) **Industrial and contracting risks** — sewage works, highway maintenance, refuse collection and disposal, large scale catering, water supply, use of heavy plant etc.

(iv) **Sporting and leisure activities** — public parks, open spaces, leisure centres, food and drink, sale of goods.

(g) **Education authorities and teachers** — Authorities, in addition to the premises risk, may become vicariously liable for the negligence of teachers of which children are the most likely and obvious victims. Teachers are in the same position as parents regarding the children under their control. In *Butt v. Cambridgeshire & Ely C.C. (1969)* a teacher was not expected to be able to deal simultaneously with all his pupils. While attending to one, an incident between two others resulted in an injury caused by scissors. However, as the following cases show liability may be the outcome of lack of supervision or danger on the premises:

Barnes v. Hants C.C. (1969) — a five year old, allowed to leave school early, was injured on the road. Held — defendants negligent.

Carmarthenshire C.C. v. Lewis (1955). A nursery school child was prepared for a walk but left alone briefly. The child went on to the road causing a lorry driver to swerve. The council was liable as a four year old child needed very close supervision.

Hamp v. St. Josephs Hospital, Mt. Carmen Convent School (1972) — an explosion in the chemistry laboratory blinded a girl. The school was liable for £76,878.

Refell v. Surrey C.C. (1964). A twelve year old put a hand through a thin pane of glass. The risk should have been foreseen.

Woodward v. Mayor of Hastings (1944). A caretaker was negligent in clearing ice from the school step. A child slipped and was injured. Defendant was held liable.

Apart from supervisory and premises aspects, there will be exposures in terms of: visitors to premises and events; school trips; food and drink risks and goods sold or supplied; motor contingent liability risk to avoid total dependence on vehicle owner's insurance.

(h) **Hospitals** — private hospitals and nursing homes run the risks of negligence of staff, premises risks, lifts, food and drink, medical treatment, dispensing and administering medicine, and contamination of ambulances.

CHAPTER 19

MISCELLANY

This chapter sets out notes on a variety of topics some of which are introduced for the first time while others take the form of recapitulation.

19.1 'Claims-made policies' and 'losses-occurring policies' compares

The hard market of the mid-1980's brought a desire on the part of insurers to shift towards 'claims-made' policies in P.L. and products covers where 'losses-occurring' policies have been the tradition. In the 'softening' market this is no longer the case and there is some shift back to losses-occurring where changes had been made. A 'claims-made' form covers claims that are first made against the insured during the period of insurance, regardless of when the injury/damage occurred. The 'losses-occurring' form covers injury/damage occurring during the period of the policy regardless of when the claim is made. The difference is of greatest consequence in the 'long-tail' claims, e.g. asbestosis, occupational deafness, pollution. Sometimes the 'claims-made' policy has a retroactive date which eliminates occurrences happening before a specific date. Some of the advantages put forward for 'claims-made' include:

(a) It is more suitable to cover pure financial loss which is not often easy to pinpoint in terms of time. (Note that when financial loss cover is added it is often in these terms even though the underlying policy may be 'losses-occurring'.)

(b) It obviates the problems of finding previous insurers in 'long-tail' cases.

(c) Policy wordings and limits are more likely to be up to date as insurers pay current claims out of current income.

(d) The greater control achieved by insurers may lead to greater stability in the market.

The disadvantages are mostly seen from the insureds' standpoint:

(a) It may be difficult at the inception to notify circumstances of claims potential, particularly in large companies where the flow of information may be such as to create difficulties.

(b) If changing from 'claims-made' to 'losses-occurring', a gap in cover arises. This necessitates the purchase of an extended reporting period (referred to as a tail) from the 'claims-made' insurer.

(c) Wordings of excess layers should be consistent with those of the primary insurance and retroactive dates should also be the same.

(d)   The 'run-off risk' provides the greatest problem. Injury/damage may have occurred but no claim notified by the time of expiry. Thus a potential uninsured loss (or series of losses as is possible in product defect cases) arises. It is possible to arrange 'extended reporting periods' and, in products liability insurance, arrange a 'batch clause' so that in a multiple claim situation, all claims resulting from the same defect will be covered by the policy in force at the time of the first claim in relation to that defect.

19.2 Excess layers

The insurer may not be prepared to provide for a limit of indemnity which is sufficient for the insured. Consequently, the insured may be compelled to purchase 'excess layers' to fill the gap created by the insufficiency of the primary insurance. For example, a person seeking professional indemnity cover may require an indemnity of £5m., achieving it by purchasing £1m. from the primary insurer and four excess layers (or some other combination) each of £1m. It is important that the excess covers should follow the wordings and, where applicable, the retroactive date of the primary insurance.

19.3 Data Protection Act 1984

The Act protects individuals from being harmed by the use of data about them held on computers and similar equipment. A breach by the data user may lead to an action for damages by an individual who suffers consequential loss. Subject to exemptions, the data user must register under the Act. Heavy fines and an order to forfeit or suffer destruction or erasure of the data can be the result of non-compliance. Liabilities (but not the fines) of the data user can be insured through legal expenses insurance or extending a professional indemnity policy.

19.4 Excesses

Large companies may, in pursuit of premium saving, seek to carry a part of the risk by excess or deductible. This can be arranged but in the field of compulsory E.L. cover it is not permitted. This, however, does not preclude an insurer from entering into an agreement with the insured whereby, after the indemnity payment, the insurer can be reimbursed up to the amount of the excess.

19.5 The American situation

Whatever problems exist in the liability market, they are always exacerbated whenever there is a U.S.A. exposure. The American courts have made some remarkable rulings. In *Zygmaniak v. Kawasaki Motors (1974)*, an injured motor-cyclist was shot dead at his own request and his widow sued the motor-cycle manufacturer for wrongful death. She succeeded, the jury holding that defects in the motor-cycle were the proximate cause of the death. Insurance premiums for products cover in the U.S.A. have increased to the extent that companies, unable to afford the premiums, have gone out of business. The following summarises 'features' of the American situation:

(a)   Strict liability in many States.

(b)   Jury awards.

(c)   Contingency fees (lawyers work on the basis that they will be paid a proportion of the award if their client's claim succeeds but nothing if it fails).

(d)   Punitive damages awarded almost routinely.

(e)   Liberal interpretation of the term 'defect'.

(f)   Reluctance to take contributory negligence into account.

(g)   Reluctance to limit the 'life' of the product (e.g. a manufacturer was held liable for a defect in a 50 year old machine which was itself second-hand).

Consequently cover for U.S.A. exports has been available on strict terms. The premium is increased on that proportion of the exports that are U.S.A. bound. Insurers may also seek to protect their position by the use of jurisdiction clauses. The pollution risk, because of onerous liability, is also difficult to insure in the States.

19.6   Global liability insurance

A global liability policy may be appropriate for a multi-national concern with highly centralised control. Under such a policy a master policy is arranged in the U.K. covering U.K. risks and applying cover world-wide. The master policy gives DIC (difference in conditions)/DIL (difference in limits) cover over local primary policies. These local policies are issued by the global insurer in each country and, where the policies fall short, the master policy, subject to its terms, fills the gap. Excess layers are placed centrally.

EXHIBIT 7

EXCESS OF LOSS REINSURANCE

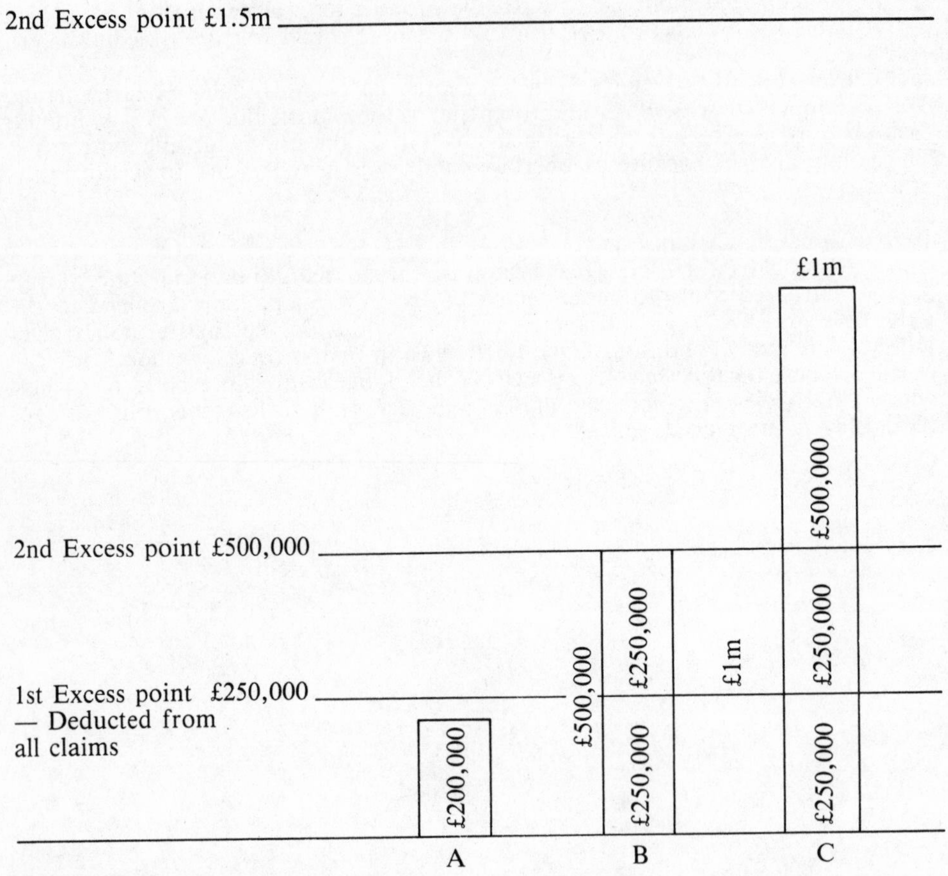

2nd Excess point £1.5m ————————————————————————

£1m

2nd Excess point £500,000 ————————————————————————

1st Excess point £250,000 ————————————————————————
— Deducted from
all claims

A   B   C

£200,000

£500,000

£250,000

£250,000

£1m

£500,000

£250,000

£250,000

Claim A — No involvement of reinsurer

Claim B — £250,000 deducted as loss retained by ceding office leaving £250,000 recovered from first layer treaty

Claim C — £250,000 retained by ceding office; £250,000 recovered under 1st layer treaty and £500,000 under 2nd layer.

In practice, more layers may exist and, in a very large loss, a claim might exceed the uppermost limit leaving the ceding office with the excess.

110

CHAPTER 20

REINSURANCE: RISK IMPROVEMENT

1. REINSURANCE

20.1　In Michigan, U.S.A. the misdelivery of a product (fire retardent instead of cattle feed) brought in its wake the death of valuable livestock, lost production, and personal injury to many people. This and other tragedies, e.g. thalidomide, are graphic reminders of the catastrophe potential in liability cases. In addition, increased claims consciousness threatens an insurer's account. To safeguard themselves against adverse results insurers seek the protection of reinsurance. In the harder market conditions of the mid-80's primary insurers have often been unwilling or unable to provide the capacity demanded by industry. One response has been to provide cover up to a level considered prudent by the insurer leaving the insured to arrange excess layers elsewhere in the market. Even insurers backed by adequate reinsurance arrangements have taken this step in order to protect the reinsurers against large potential claims and thus protect their own reinsurance arrangements. Another approach is to set up a scheduled policy on a co-insurance basis.

20.2　**Co-insurance.** In a scheduled policy a number of insurers share the risk on an agreed basis. Five insurers, for example, might share the risk on the basis that the leader takes 30%; three others take 20% each and the fifth takes 10%. Documentation etc. is handled by the lead office but claims are shared in the agreed proportions. The insured has a direct contractual relationship with each participating insurer who is directly liable to the insured for their own share of the loss. Each insurer is likely to have its own reinsurance arrangements to spread the risk still further.

20.3　**Reinsurance.** In reinsurance there is no direct relationship between the insured and the reinsurer. The insured has a right of claim against the primary insurer only. Reinsurance in the liability field is generally by treaty and on a non-proportional basis.

20.4　**Excess of loss treaties.** This is non-proportional. The insurer fixes the limit (i.e. the excess point of his choice). In the event of a claim, the ceding office pays up to the limit which, when exceeded, entitles the office to recover the excess, subject to an upper limit not being exceeded, under the reinsurance treaty. For example, given an excess point of £100,000 and an upper limit £250,000, a claim of £200,000 will be shared equally between the ceding office and the reinsurer. To cover the situation when the upper limit is exceeded additional layers are arranged. As most claims are in the lower region, the reinsurance rate decreases as the layers move upwards. The ceding office may decide to take a further part of the risk in the higher areas by taking a layer between, say the second and third treaties. The premium charged by reinsurers is based on the actual experience of the ceding office plus administration costs. It is known as the burning cost method.

20.5   Stop loss treaties. These, sometimes called excess of loss ratio, unlike excess of loss, which focuses on the individual claim, are concerned with the overall account. The treaty limits claims in the aggregate to a predetermined percentage of premium income. However, the reinsurer does not accept responsibility for all of the excess as to do so would be to risk imprudent underwriting by the ceding office. The latter, therefore, is made a co-insurer in the excess. The following question and answer illustrate and compare the two treaties described.

Company X writes a small portfolio of liability business. In 1986, X's premium income was £440,000 but claims for the period were £470,000. No claims were outstanding. The 5 largest claims were settled for: £9,500, £12,000, £12,500, £16,000 and £20,000 respectively. X had an excess of loss treaty for the excess of £10,000. Show the reinsurance recovery by X and say whether it would have been better or worse if instead of excess of loss treaty, X has effected stop loss reinsurance based on 75% of 90% of gross premium income. Assume that no upper limits in the treaty will be exceeded.

FIVE LOSSES	EXCESS POINT	RECOVERY
1. £9,500	£10,000	NIL
2. £12,000	£10,000	£2,000
3. £12,500	£10,000	£2,500
4. £16,000	£10,000	£6,000
5. £20,000	£10,000	£10,000
		£20,500 Total recovered

Gross premium income = £440,000

90% thereon = £396,000

total claims = £470,000

£74,000 difference

75% of £74,000 =   £55,500 Total recovered

Therefore X's result would be better with the stop-loss treaty.

20.6   Other treaties. A quota share treaty is one where the ceding office agrees to cede a specified proportion of every risk within a particular category regardless of limits of indemnity. It means sharing even the smaller risks with the reinsurer and is most likely to be suitable for a small but growing company. A surplus treaty operates when the ceding offices identifies a point up to which they will retain the entire risk and seek reinsurance whereby its shares proportionately risks in excess of that retention. The larger the risk, the smaller the retention becomes as a proportion and claims are shared proportionately.

20.7   Facultative reinsurance. This involves separate negotiation and takes place to accommodate risks that are outside the scope of treaty arrangements.

20.8 **Stability index clause.** This is used to safeguard the reinsurer against the effects of inflation. In the interval between the creation of the treaty and the settlement of the claim inflation could seriously affect the amount of the claim. If the ceding office's excess point remained unadjusted then all of the effects of inflation would fall upon the reinsurer while the real value of the insuring office's loss would be reduced. Indeed some claims, if settled at the time of occurrence, might have been wholly within the excess point but inflation by time of settlement pushes them beyond it. An insurer's retention might be £40,000 with excess of loss above that figure. Notification of a claim in year one generates a reserve of £30,000. Settlement might take four years when £46,000 is paid. In the absence of the clause the reinsurer would pay £6,000 whereas if settlement had been earlier at the reserved figure the reinsurer would have escaped liability. The clause introduces an index linked to prices (or some other indicator) so that the retention will be increased in line with increases in the index. Assume that in year one of the example the index stood at 120 and by the time of settlement it reached 132. The effect would be:

Insurers retention	£40,000
Claim paid	£46,000
Index at loss date	120
Index at settlement	132

The calculation would be:

$$\text{Retention } £40,000 \times \frac{132}{120} = £44,000$$

Therefore the insurer pays £44,000 and the reinsurer pays £2,000 with the result that the ceding office bears its share of the effects of inflation.

20.9 **Pooling.** This arises with very onerous risks and is the result of an agreement between several insurers to form a pool into which are paid the premiums received by all members for that class of business and from which all claims and expenses will be paid. Liability insurance for nuclear reactor operators is an example of a pooling arrangement.

2. RISK IMPROVEMENT

20.10 The primary purpose of liability insurance is to provide an indemnity for the financial burden for injury and damage caused by the activities of the insured. The costs of accidents in industry, commerce and professional life are heavy and show no signs of abating. Insurers take an objective interest in the work of accident prevention and the reduction in accident waste. Quite apart from those aspects that can be expressed in monetary terms (e.g. compensation payable and costs and expenses in handling claims), there are other less obvious costs. Indeed the very presence of risk provokes a costly reaction which takes many forms. Risk avoidance may be the most costly reaction of all so that firms who incurred risks in manufacturing new and much-needed pharmaceutical products might decide to go for low risks products such as aspirins, thus causing society to forgo the benefits from the

113

new products. Risk prevention and reduction consumes resources as do the services of the police, fire and ambulance services to say nothing of the insurance industry itself. The role of risk improvement falls upon all concerned including the government and industry itself. The insurance industry provides an accident prevention service to its customers as do leading brokers. Sometimes the service is free or a fee may be charged.

20.11 Insurance Surveys. By carrying out surveys and making recommendations insurers contribute to accident prevention. The insured should benefit in terms of avoiding the disruption and consumption of time that follows an accident. Also he should benefit in terms of lower premiums. Smaller risks may not be surveyed but when undertaken, qualified and experienced personnel from the insurance industry coming in and taking an outsider's view, can often identify features overlooked by the insured and his staff who concentrate their attention on other aspects of their business. The surveyor will look at (from an EL standpoint): the record of accidents; general factory conditions; details of machines; welfare and protective clothing; training aspects; first-aid; accident prevention measures and compliance with statutes and regulations etc. Industrial relations are also a matter of relevance the surveyor may comment upon. In the P.L. survey the emphasis on the risks faced by third parties and it must be ascertained how they come into contact with the insured's activities.

20.12 Information and advice. Insurers as individual companies or as members of associations make a substantial contribution to accident prevention by way of literature, research, films and advice.

CII examination report 1987

This report, prepared by the CII's examiners, is intended to help students and teachers in preparing for the examinations by giving an indication of the points which should have been brought out in answers and also examiners' comments on how candidates actually performed in the examinations.

The report shows the main points or headings which examiners were seeking in answer to each question (candidates would be expected to expand upon these points). These are not model answers and should not be regarded as such. There may not indeed be any right or wrong answer to some of the questions, so in cases where candidates displayed imagination and originality, examiners gave them credit even though the answers were not along the lines expected.

Great care is taken in the setting of all papers. For each subject there is a senior examiner who is required to present the paper he has set to a panel of experts and an assessor. Each paper is carefully scrutinised to ensure that there are no ambiguities, errors or inconsistencies and that the paper is generally fair. Assessors and examiners are carefully selected from the insurance industry for their technical expertise and experience and they must be sympathetic to the educational philosophy of the Institute and the needs of the students.

The Institute cannot enter into any correspondence about the suggested main points for the answers.

CII Tuition Servie study courses include a copy of the latest report. Other 1987 reports can also be obtained separately and most of the 1986 reports are still available; the cost is £1 a copy.

ARRANGEMENT

All matter reproduced from the question paper itself is enclosed in boxes. After the heading and examination instructions in a box running the full width of the page, the examiners' comments appear in italic type on how well the candidates performed in the examination in dealing with the paper as a whole. Each question is then treated separately: first the question itself is printed in a box, then a brief statement of the points that the examiners expected candidates to deal with in their answers, and finally, in italic type, the examiners' comments on how well candidates answered the question in the examination.

---

070. Insurances of liability

Three hours are allowed for this paper. Answer SIX questions only. All questions carry equal marks.

Examiners considered this paper to be a little more straightfoward than those of previous years. However, while there was a reduction in the number of candidates falling well below marks of 50 per cent, there does not seem to have been a corresponding increase in the numbers achieving more than 50 per cent. Thus while candidates in answering some questions were able to gain fairly high marks, in the main this only balanced deficiencies in knowledge shown in the answers to other questions. In these latter questions there was ample evidence of candidates not reading or considering questions sufficiently before answering. Some overseas students produced very poor answers but others (probably from different locations) wrote very good answers and showed both theoretical and practical knowledge.

QUESTION 1

An animal feed manufacturer sho has the usual form of products liability cover receives the following claims:
- *(a)* A farmer's cattle become ill after eating the feed, due to a mistake made in that particular farmer's consignment.
- *(b)* Dust from the feed explodes in the warehouse of the manufacturer's factory. An employee of the manufacturer is injured and also the driver of a third party vehicle.
- *(c)* A farmer alleges that the feed has failed to fatten his cattle although he followed all recommendations.
- *(d)* A purchaser of the feed reports that it has deteriorated in storage. All instructions have been followed.

Explain in each case whether there is a valid claim under the products liability cover.

a. This is the type of claim the product liability cover is meant to meet. There was only a mistake in the claimant's consignment and there is no question of the faulty design or formula exclusion applying if there is one.
b. Employees of the insured are excluded under the products policy and a claim should be made under the employer's liability policy.

The third party driver has been injured by goods still in the custody or control of the insured and so the claim should be handled by the manufacturer's public liability policy.
c. This type of product liability policy would probably have an efficacy clause excluding the unsuitability of the goods for the purpose for which they were designed. Such cover is given by a products guarantee policy if obtainable.
d. The only damage in this case is to the product itself so no cover applies. There is no third party damage so there is no liability under the policy. There is no cover for the replacement of defective goods if that is argued. Even if the instructions were faulty this would also be excluded by the formula or design exclusion. However, not every products policy has a faulty design or formula exclusion. Pure economic loss is excluded as it does not arise from loss or damage to property which is covered.

This was generally well answered with the exception of part (d). Quite a number of candidates considered the claim in (d) was excluded becaue of inherent vice of the product, rather than loss or damage to the product itself being excluded. The question of faulty instructions and the application of the design exclusion was not considered by the majority. The tendency to write introductory paragraphs on the products policy generally was unnecessary.

QUESTION 2

Jones & Co. who hold separate employers' and public liabiliyt policies, have agreed with the local education authority to accept senior school pupils for a course of training and work experience. They will work under supervision but will not receive wages from Jones & Co. The education authority has asked Jones & Co. to confirm that the trainees will be 'fully insured whilst under the direction of the firm'. To what extent will each of Jones & Co.'s policies meet this requirement?

In the first place the trainees are not fully insured as the employers' and public liability policies only cover legal liability.

The employers' liability policy will cover Jones & Co.'s liability to trainees in the course of their work or training, although they are not engaged under a contract of service. This type of policy is normally extended (or can be if rquired) to treat these trainees as though they were employees for the purpose of the policy. This policy would also respond if an employee is injured through the negligence of a trainee.

If the employers' liability policy has been extended as above, the public liability policy will exclude injury to trainees in these circumstances but will cover the liability of the firm (or of the trainee) for injury to third parties or loss of or damage to third party property. If the employers' liability and public liability policies are with the same insurer this overlap in cover will no doubt be avoided but might be overlooked if the policies are with different insurers.

This was one of the less popular questions. Few appreciated the implications of the term 'fully insured' and even fewer considered the problems that could arise if the employers' and public liability policies were with different insurers. There was an over-emphasis on the legal, rather than the policy definition of an employee.

QUESTION 3

Explain the term 'vicarious liability'. In what circumstances does such liability arise?

Vicarious liability arises when one party has to assume responsibility for the torts of another and the dictu, *Qui facit per alium facit per se* (he who acts through another acts himself) is the guiding principle in these cases. These liabilities for the consequences of another's negligence arise from business and other special relationships existing between the person who commits the negligence and the person held responsible. The relationship gives the latter, as a general rule, a degree of control over the former's actions, and this carries with it responsibility for a wrongful act of neglect. It also means that the plaintiff is free to sue both parties. There will also be the right of the party vicariously liable to seek an indemnity from the actual perpetrator of the act in question.

There are four main categories of vicarious liability:
a. employer/employee or master/servant (the health authority's liability for the acts of doctors although not a master/servant relationship is another example);
b. principal/agent;
c. principal/independent contractor;
d. partners.

The former is responsible for the latter's actions in (a) in all cases arising out of and in the course of the employee's employment; (b) in cases arising out of the agent acting within his authority; and (c) in certain circumstances only. Partners are liable jointly and separately for torts committed by any co-partner in the ordinary course of the business of the firm or with the authority of the co-partners (Partnership Act 1890).

This was one of the most popular questions and on the whole was well answered. Some answers were slanted towards specific examples to the detriment of an explanation of underlying principles. Also there was a tendency to dwell on the one relationship and generalities of levels of responsibility and control in vicarious liability situations. Parent and child was wrongly given as a relationship involving vicarious liability.

QUESTION 4

Jones, intending to dine at an hotel, parked his car in the hotel car park. His coat was taken from him by a waiter. When he had finished his meal he found his coat was missing from the coat rack. He complained to the manager who stated that the hotel was not responsible for the customers' coats and pointed to a disclaimer notice above the coat rack. Jones went out of the hotel to find that his car was missing. The manager explained that the hotel was not responsible for customers' cars. Jones then stormed out tripping over a suitcase that had been left in the middle of the foyer by the hall porter. He broke his ankle. What are his legal remedies? Give your reasons.

As Jones did not book sleeping accommodation, the Hotel Proprietors' Act 1956 does not apply. In any event, this Act does not apply to vehicles or any property left therein. However, a hotel proprietor can stil be held liable for such loss or damage if negligence can be established against him. Nevertheless, as in this case Jones himself parked the car and the keys were not given to a hall porter to park it, the probability is that the hotel manager is correct in denying liability. There may even be a notice of disclaimer in the car park which Jones knew about or should have known about and thus accepted its terms which would put the matter beyond any doube.

A hotel would not normally be responsible for the loss of coats belonging to non-residents provided notice of this is given to the customer. In this case, Jones did not deposit his coat personally but allowed it to be taken by a member of the hotel staff. The hotel as bailees would then be liable for the loss.

Turning to the injury Jones suffered, it is a borderline case. Jones should have looked where he was going and in that respect was guilty of a degree of contributory negligence. However, the management should not allow obstacles to be left in places where customers are likely to fall over them. Jones would probably obtain some damages for this negligence.

Not many candidates realised that the Hotel Proprietors' Act did not apply. Thus they tended to start off on the wrong foot. Howver, the role of the disclaimer notice was usually appreciated but not that the hotel was in the position of a bailee regarding the coat. Some candidates actually confused disclaimer notices with the statutory notice required by the Act.

QUESTION 5

Under the Contractors' Plant Association's Model Conditions for the hiring of plant (1979), if the hird plant is lost or damaged in the following circumstances hich party to this contract is responsible and why?
(a) Malicious damage by vandals when on the hirer's site.
(b) Accidental damage in transit to the hirer's site.
(c) Accidental damage during the erection of the plant on site.
(d) Loss in a marsh on the site area due to negligence by the owner's driver.
(e) Accidental damage while unloading at site because of the fault of the owner's personnel.

a. The hirer is responsible for malicious damage by vandals because he accepts this under clause 13. That he took all reasonable precautions is no excuse — the condition is strict.

b. The owner is responsible for damage, loss or injury due to, or arising before, delivery of any plant to the site of the hirer where the plant is in transit by transport of the owner or as otherwise arranged by the owner, by sub-clause 13(c),(i).

c. The owner is responsible under sub-clause 13(c),(ii) provided such erection is under the exclusive control of the owner or his agent.

d. The hirer is responsible for the handling of the plant unless an incompetent, as distinct from a negligent driver is supplied, by clauses 8 and 13(b). Clause 8 states that drivers or operators shall, for all purposes in connection with their employment in the working of the plant, be regarded as the servants or agents of the hirer. *Phillips Products* v. *Hamstead Plant Hire* (1983 *concerning clause 8 being unreasonable under the Unfair Contract Terms Act 1977 is porobably limited to its own facts.*

e. The hirer is responsible under clause 4 (loading and unloading) which states that any personnel supplied by the owner shall be deemed to be under the hirer's control and shall comply with all directions of the hirer.

Candidates did not seem to have a good knowledge of the CPA Conditions. It was not a popular question and was not well answered because there was not enough detail given to obtain good marks. There was too much reliance on 'yes' or 'no' answers.

QUESTION 6

Explain briefly the liability insurances required by a large firm manufacturing biscuits.

The following liability insurances would provide adequate protection for a biscuit manufacturer:

—general public liability policy: covers legal liability for injury to third parties or their property arising from the conduct of the business. A limit of indemnity applies in respect of each occurence or series of occurrences arising out of one event;

—product liability policy: cover in respect of liability for goods sold or supplies is excluded from the basic general liability policy but can be provided by an extension or the issue of a separate policy. The limit of indemnity applies in the aggregate for the period of the insurance;

—employers' liability policy: covers legal liability of the employer for death or injury to employees arising out of, and in the course of, their employment and is compulsory in the United Kingdom. The indemnity is unlimited;

—motor policy: covers legal liability for injury or damage to third parties or their property, including passengers, arising out of the use of any commercial motor vehicles used for supply, delivery or other purposes in connection with the business. There is no limit of indemnity in respect of injuries but a limit per accident is applied in respect of property damage. A fleet policy would also be required for the private cars of commercial travellers. If employees use their own vehicles on their employer's business a separate policy covering the employer's continuing liability would be desirable. Except for the contingency cover the injury to third parties aspect of these policies is compulsory cover in the UK;

—engineering policies: cover for legal liability to third parties in connection with such plant as steam baking ovens, mechanical dough mixtures and kneaders, boilers, lighting apparatus, etc., could be provided under these policies or the cover could be provided under the general public liability policy.

All the above policies will, in addition to indemnifying the insured in respect of damages, pay any costs and expenses awarded to a third party and the insured's own legal costs and expenses incurred with the insurer's consent. It is necessary to ensure that adequate limits of indemnity are selected.

A large firm manufacturing biscuits would probably have a large measure of self-insurance on public and products liability thus controlling the handling of small- to medium-size claims.

This was a popular question which was reasonably well answered. Surprisingly some candidates missed the liability cover under motor policies and in other cases adequate details of the various liability insurances wree omitted, eg, limits of indemnity.

QUESTION 7

Alfred entered Tom's shop and asked for a bottle of a well-known patent aphid destroyer. Tom said he was out of stock. Alfred explained about the greenfly on his tomato plants and asked Tom to suggest something else. Tom showed him something called 'The All-Purpose Plant Spray' which according to the label (which Alfred read) claimed to destroy aphids. Alfred purchased it and used it. It destroyed the tomato plants.

Alfred sued Tom for damages. Explain the legal position.

This is a sale by description under the Sale of Goods Act 1979. Under s.14(3) of this Act where the seller sells goods in the course of a business and the buyer expressly, or by implication, makes known to the seller any particular purpose for which the goods are being bought, there is an implied condition that the goods supplied under the contract are reasonably fit for that purpose.

Clearly in the case in question, Alfred made known to Tom the particular purpose for which the goods were being bought. In *Baldrey* v. *Marshall* (1925) Baldrey asked a firm of motor dealers for a car that would be suitable for touring and they recommended a Bugatti. A contract of sale was entered into for a Bugatti but after he had used it, Baldrey found that it was not suitable for touring purposes. The Court of Appeal has no hesitation in holding that the dealers were in breach of the condition that the car should be fit for Baldrey's purpose. A more recent case illustrating this point is *Ashington Piggeries* v. *Christopher Hill* (1971).

Under s.14(2) there is also an implied condition that goods are of merchantable quality except where goods are examined by the purchaser, which should reveal any defects. Obviously there were no defects apparent to Alfred when he examined the bottle in Tom's shop so the exception cannot apply. In the case in question Tom's judgment was obviously relied on. The goods were not fit for use or else they were not of merchantable quality. It is unlikely that the fact that Alfred read the label would affect Tom's liability for breach of condition and he would be obliged to pay damages, unless Alfred was guilty of incorrectly following the instructions.

While the manufacturer of the spray is liable for his negligence it is easier for Alfred as buyer to proceed against Tom as seller, as mentioned above, leaving Tom as buyer to recover from his seller (who may be the manufacturer or wholesaler).

The EEC Directive on Product Liability does not apply to property of small value.

This question was answered as well as was expected. This was basically a question on section 14 of the Sale of Goods Act but it was not always answered on this basis and those who did were often not familiar with its implications, thus marks tended to be low. Some based their answers on professional negligence and even seemed to think that caveat emptor *still applied.*

QUESTION 8

Define nuisance and state briefly the conditions that have to exist before there is liability for nuisance.

Nuisance has been defined as a wrong done to a man by unlawfully disturbing him in the enjoyment of his property or, in some cases, in the exercise of a common right. There are two kinds of nuisance — public and private. The former does not fall within the law of torts except that a particular case may constitute some liability in

117

which event it is actionable by an individual if it causes him special damage over and above the inconvenience suffered by other members of the public. In *Fisher* v. *Ruislip-Northwood UDC* (1945) a car came into collision with an unlit air-raid shelter and the defendants were held liable. On the other hand a car does not constitute a nuisance immediately it breaks down unforeseeably. A more recent case is *Tate and Lyle Industries* v. *GLC* (1983) where the construction of ferry terminals by the GLC and the consequent silting of the waterway, which prevented the navigation of vessels, constituted a public nuisance.

Private nuisances are interferences for a substantial length of time by other with the owner's or occupier's use or enjoyment of property — see *Cunard* v. *Antifyre* (1932). Such a nuisance may be the wrongful disturbance of rights attaching to land or the act of wrongfully causing or allowing the escape of noxious things such as smoke, smells, noise and the like.

The conditions that have to be satisfied before there can be liability are two — *injuria* and *damnum*. The former refers to a wrongful act which constitutes or causes damage, while the latter is the damage, loss or inconvenience actually suffered.

Normally the right of action vests solely in the occupier and does not extend to the owner or other people who, although lawfully on the premises, are not in legal possession. In *Malone* v. *Laskey* (1907), the occupier's wife was injured by the fall of a cistern due to vibration set up by the defendant's machinery but it was held that she had no cause of action for nuisance.

This question was generally well answered. Most candidates could define and explain nuisance and were aware of the two forms. Too few set out the conditions necessary, ie, injuria *and* damnum, *preferring to talk about defences. Also few candidates mentioned the individuals who have this right of action.*

INDEX